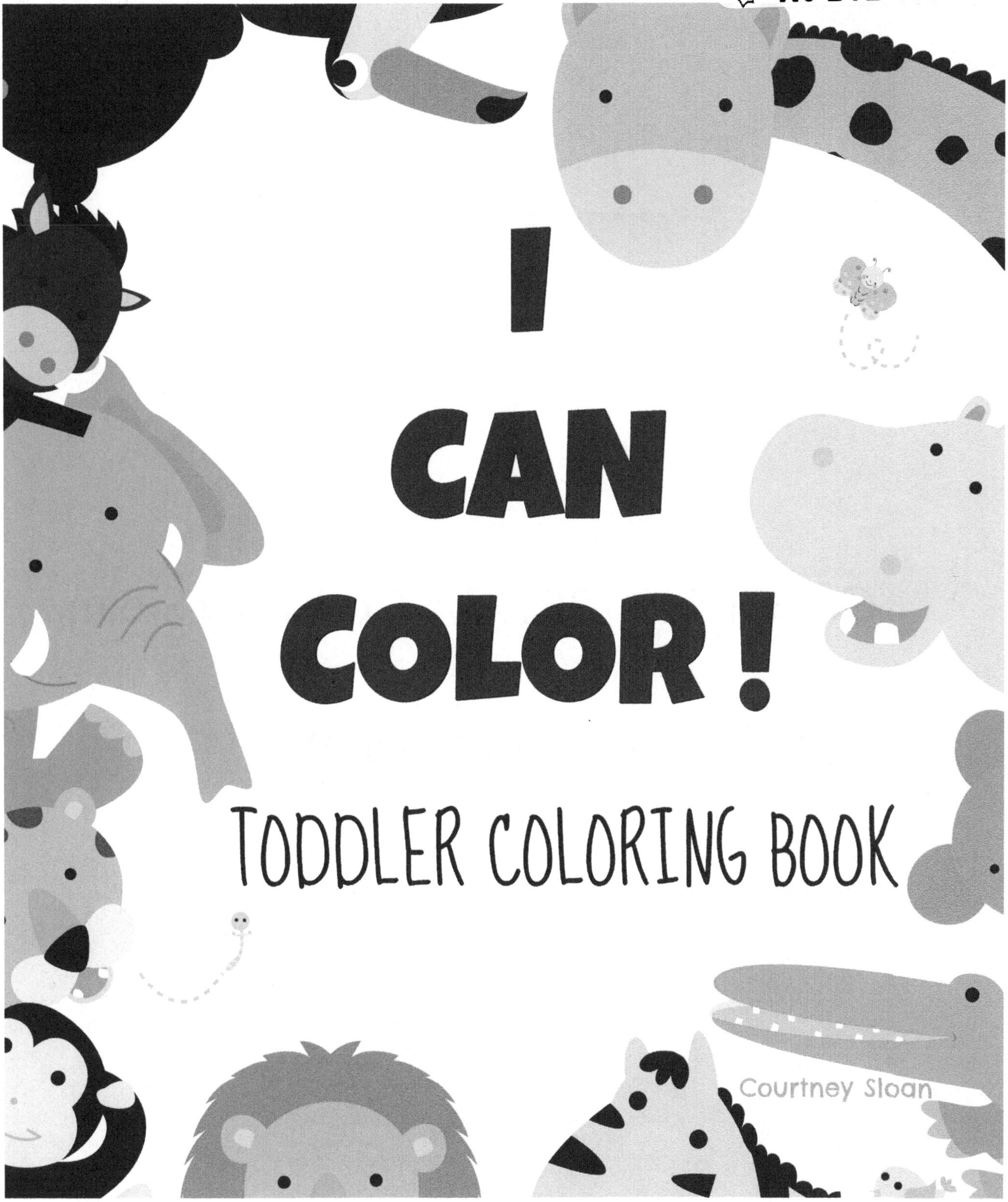

I CAN COLOR!

TODDLER COLORING BOOK

Courtney Sloan

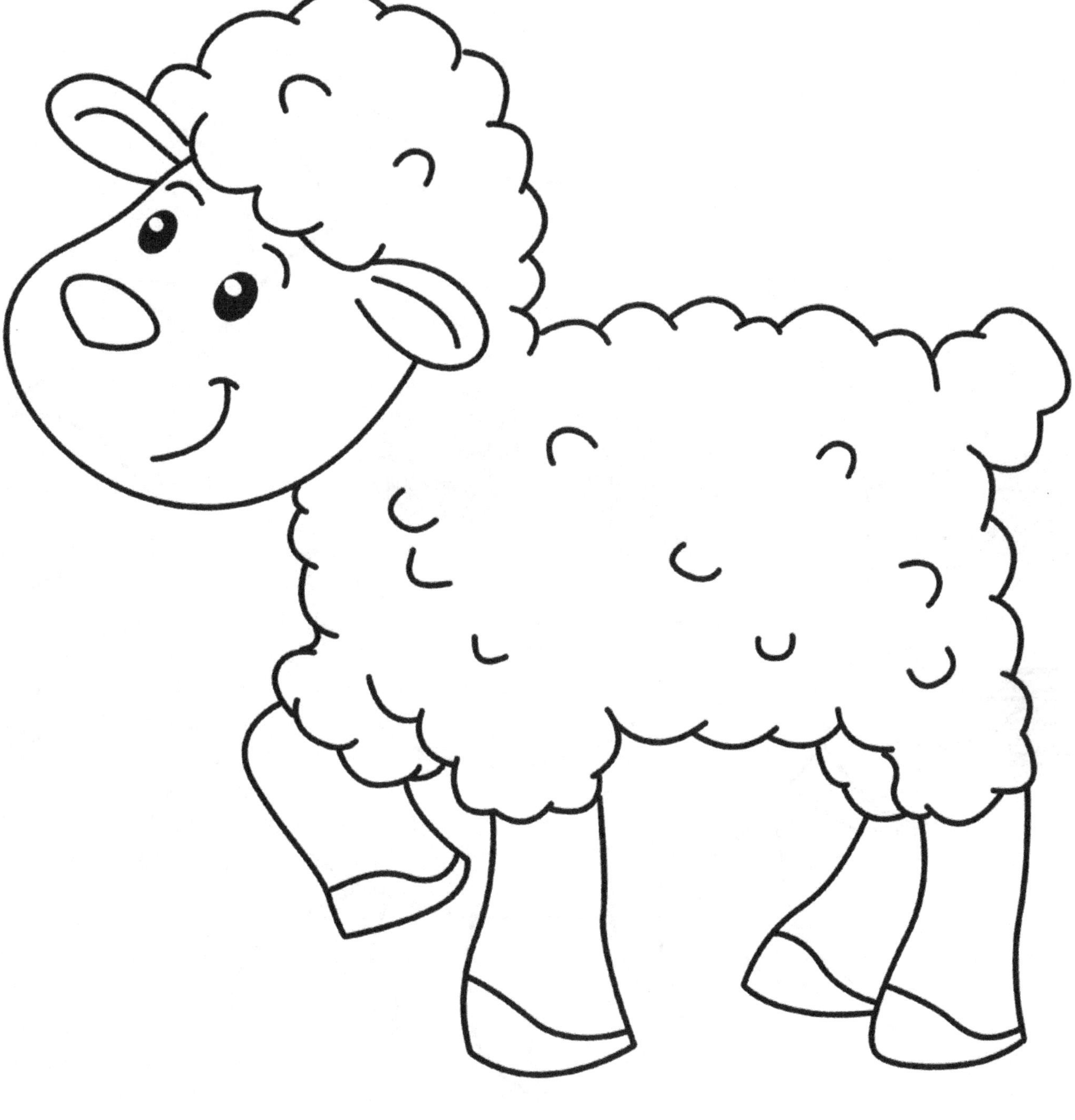

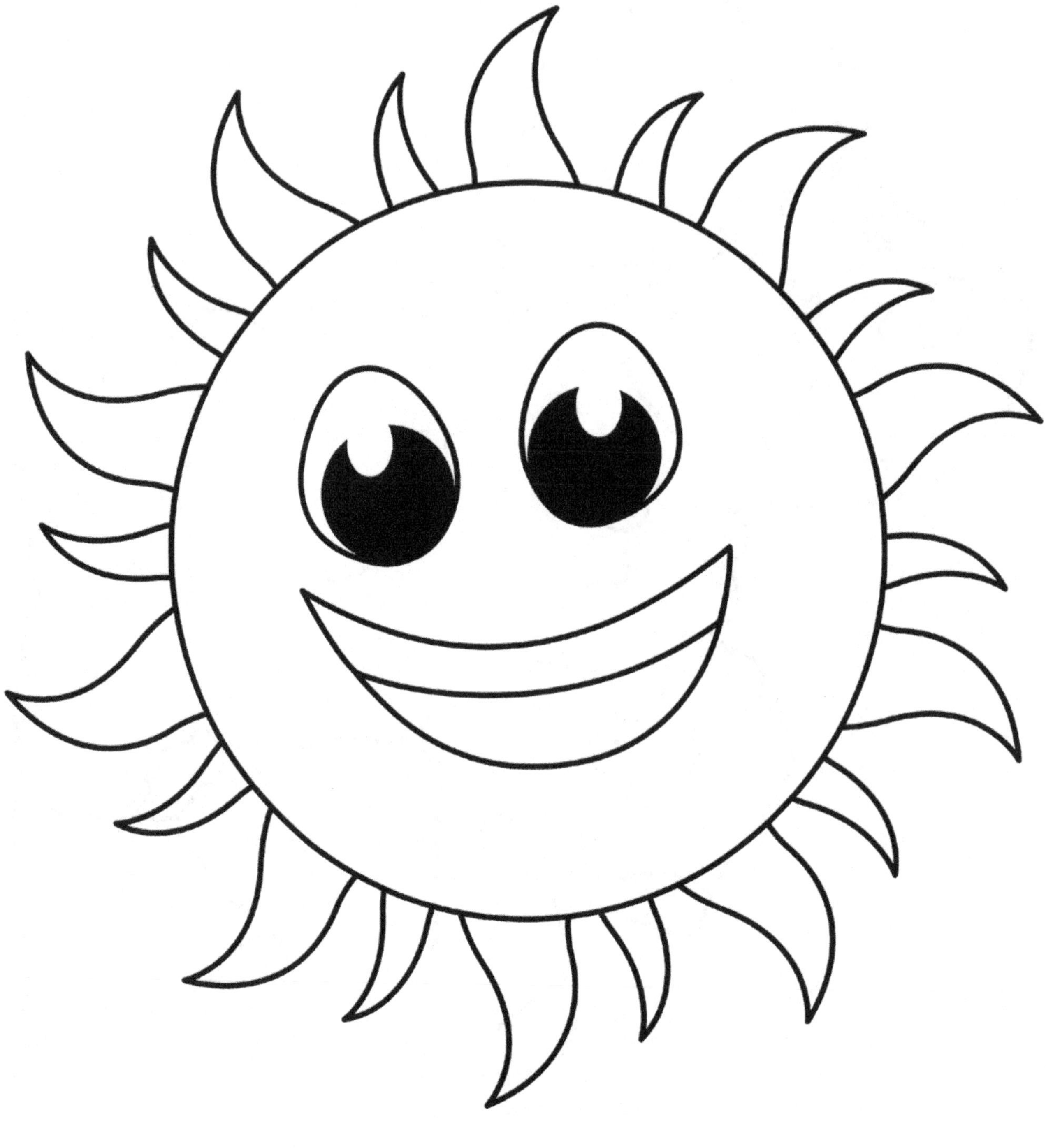

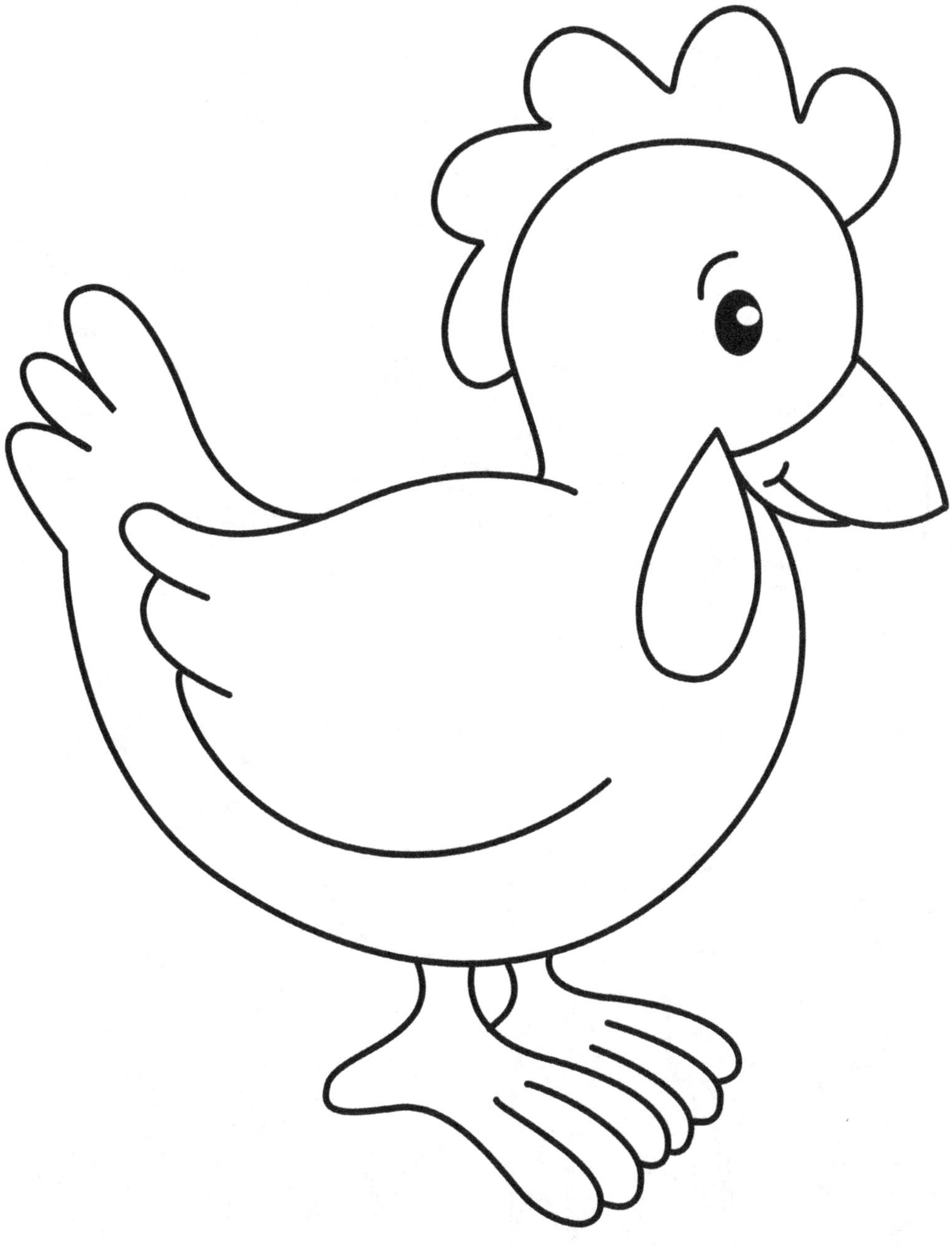

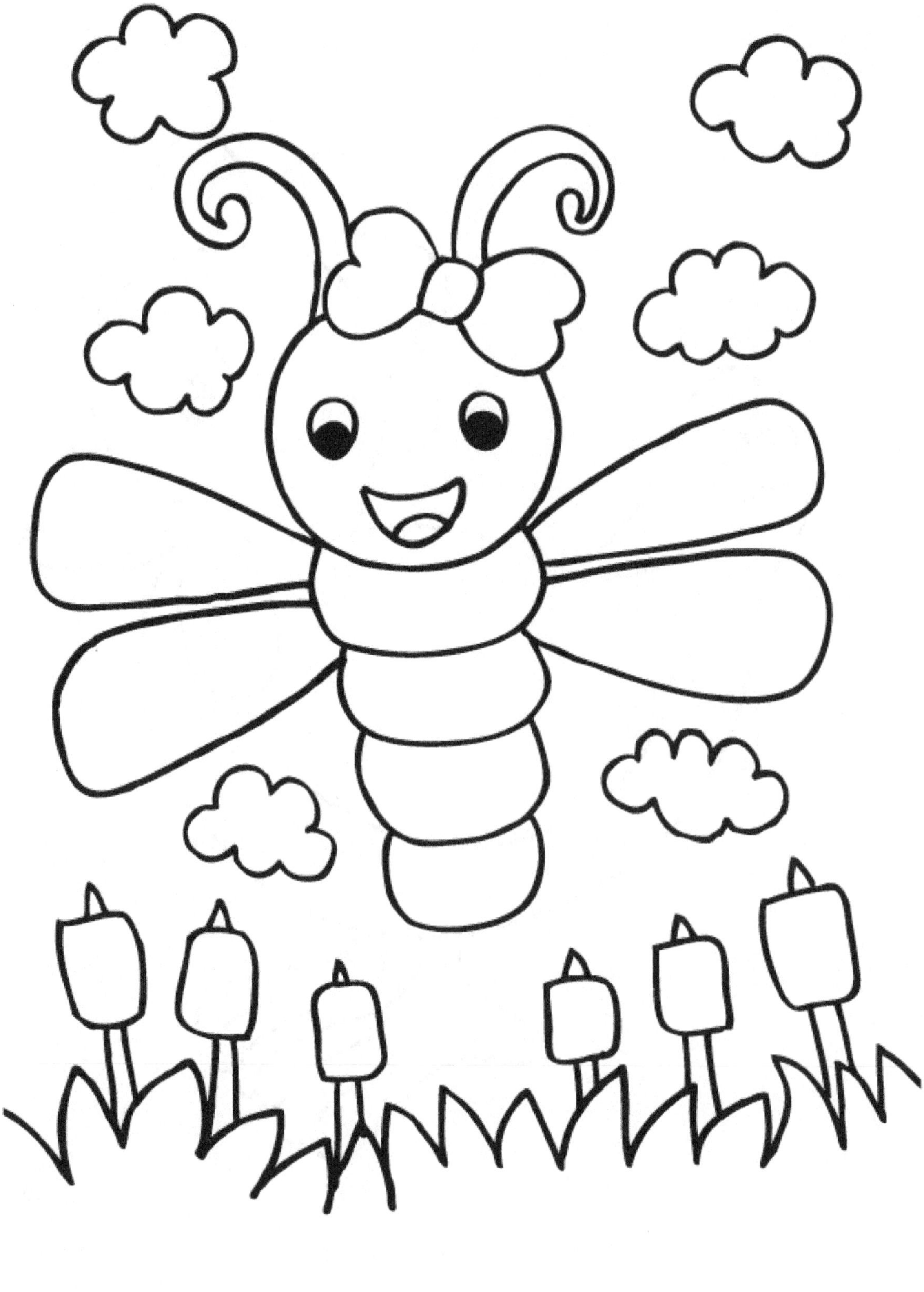

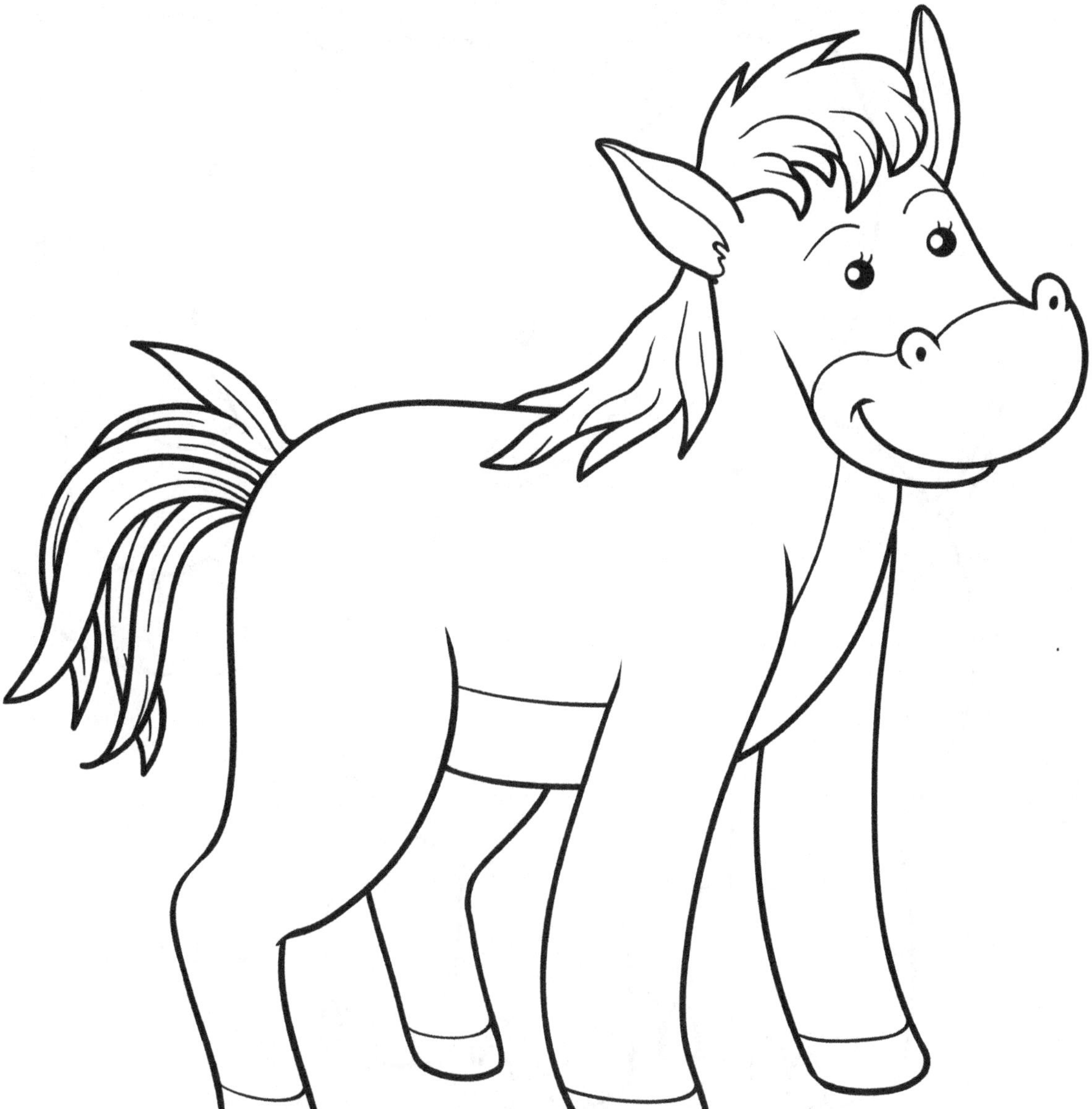

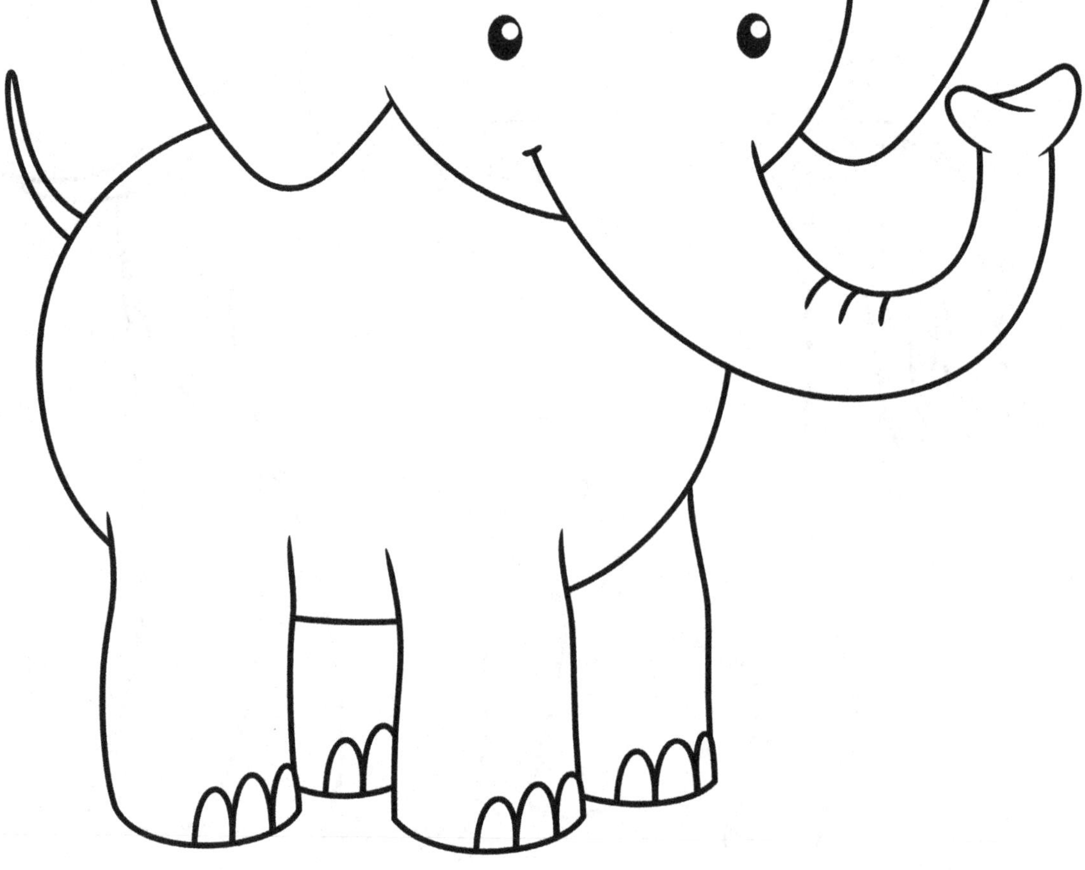

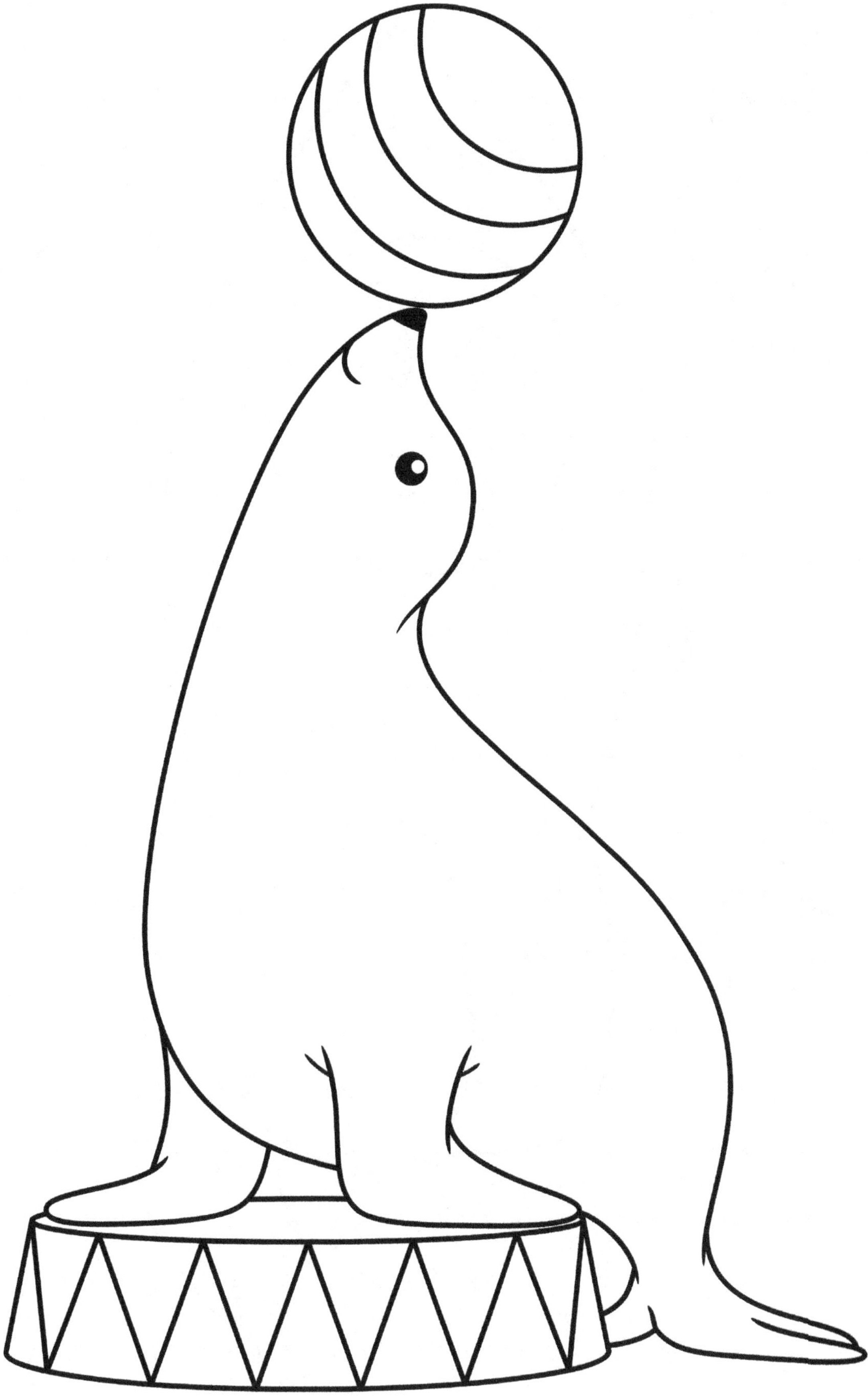

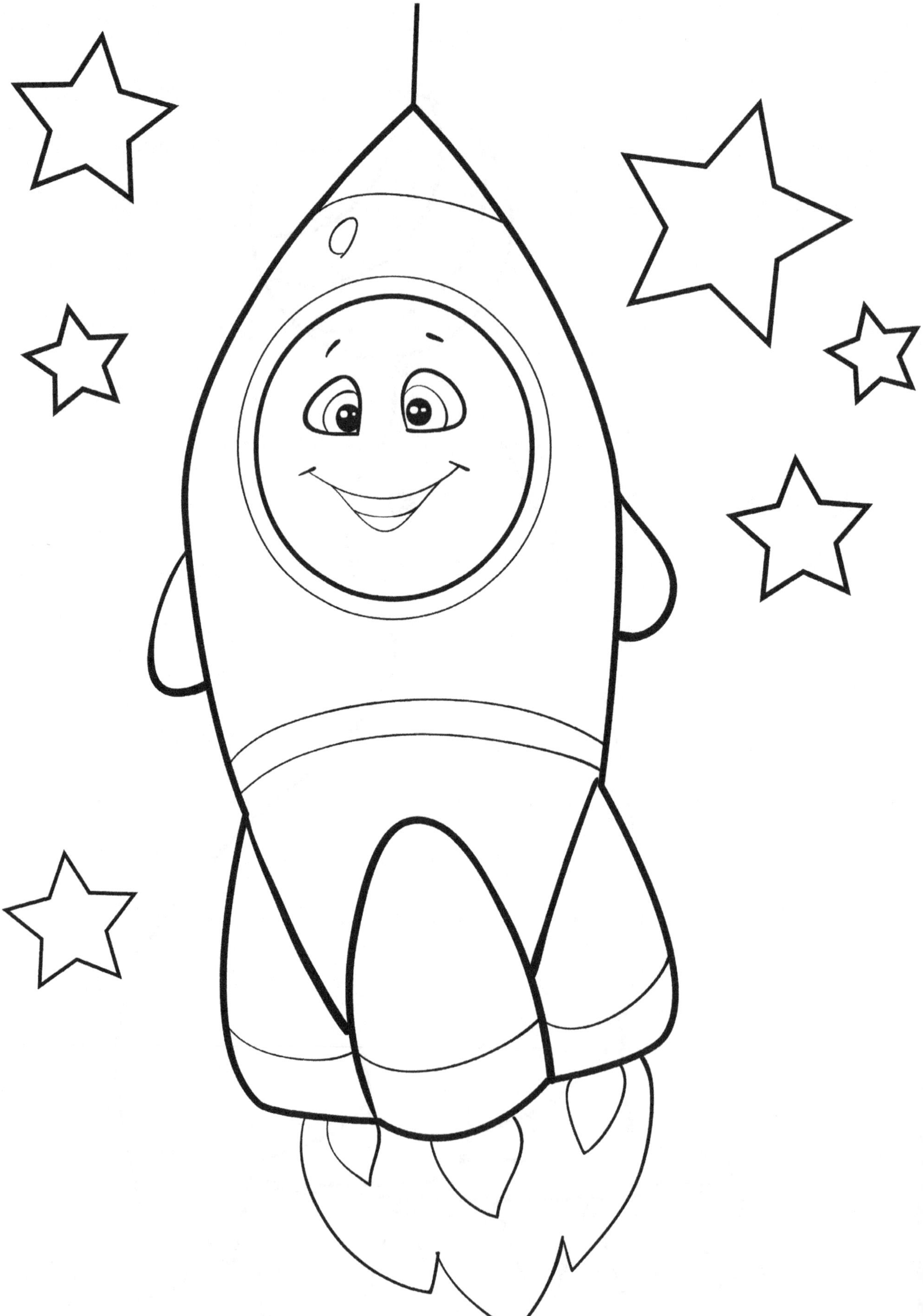

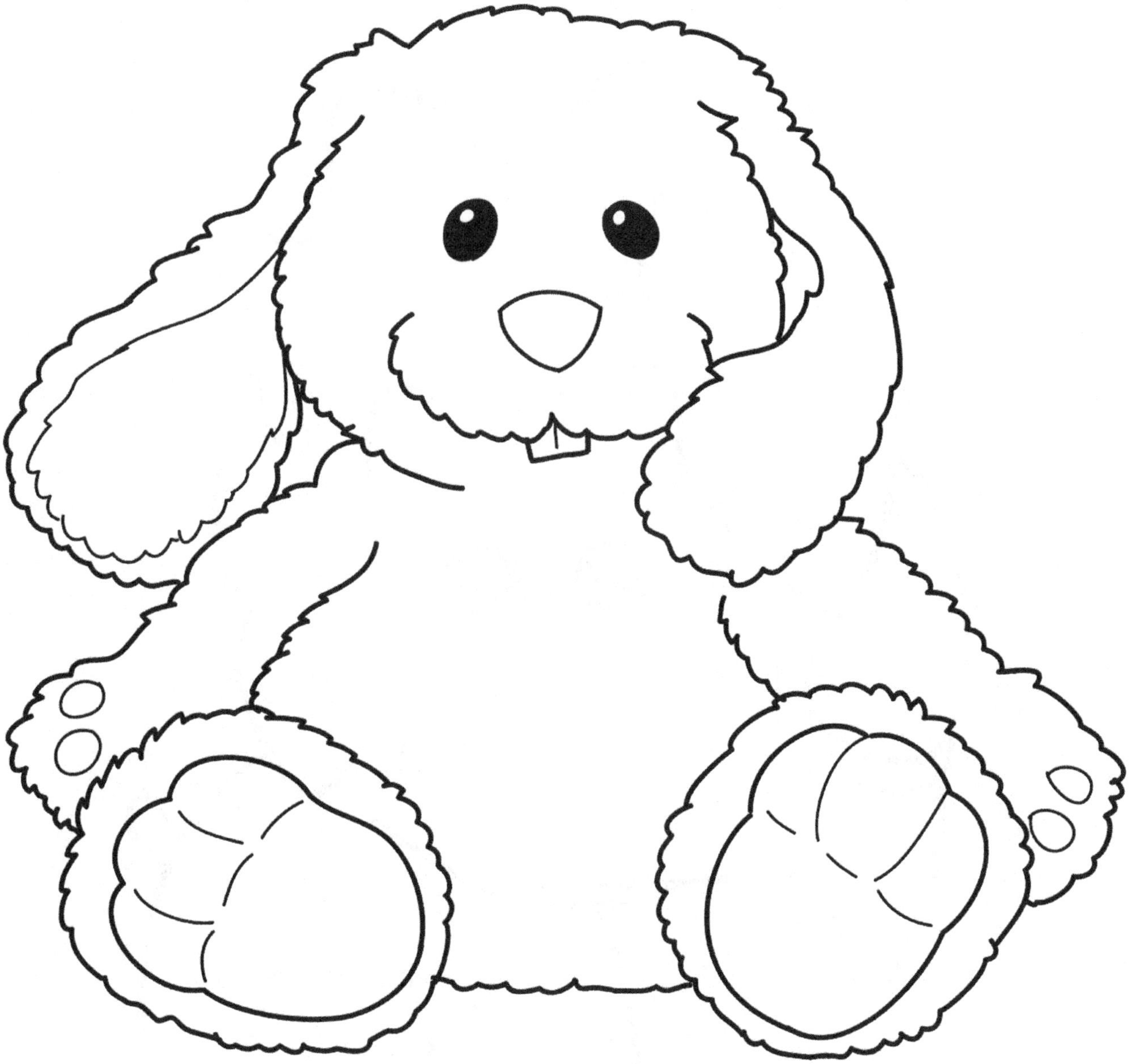

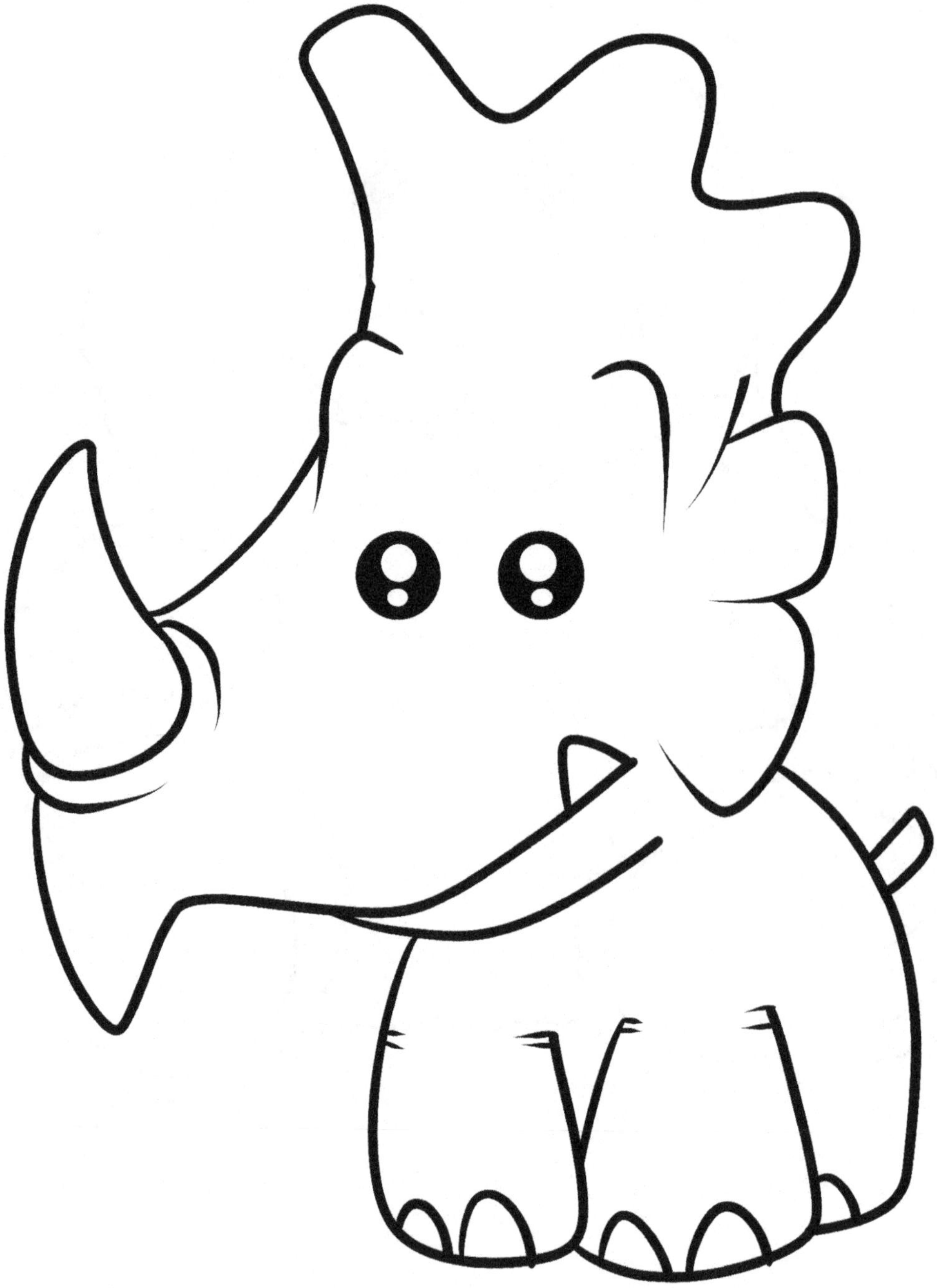

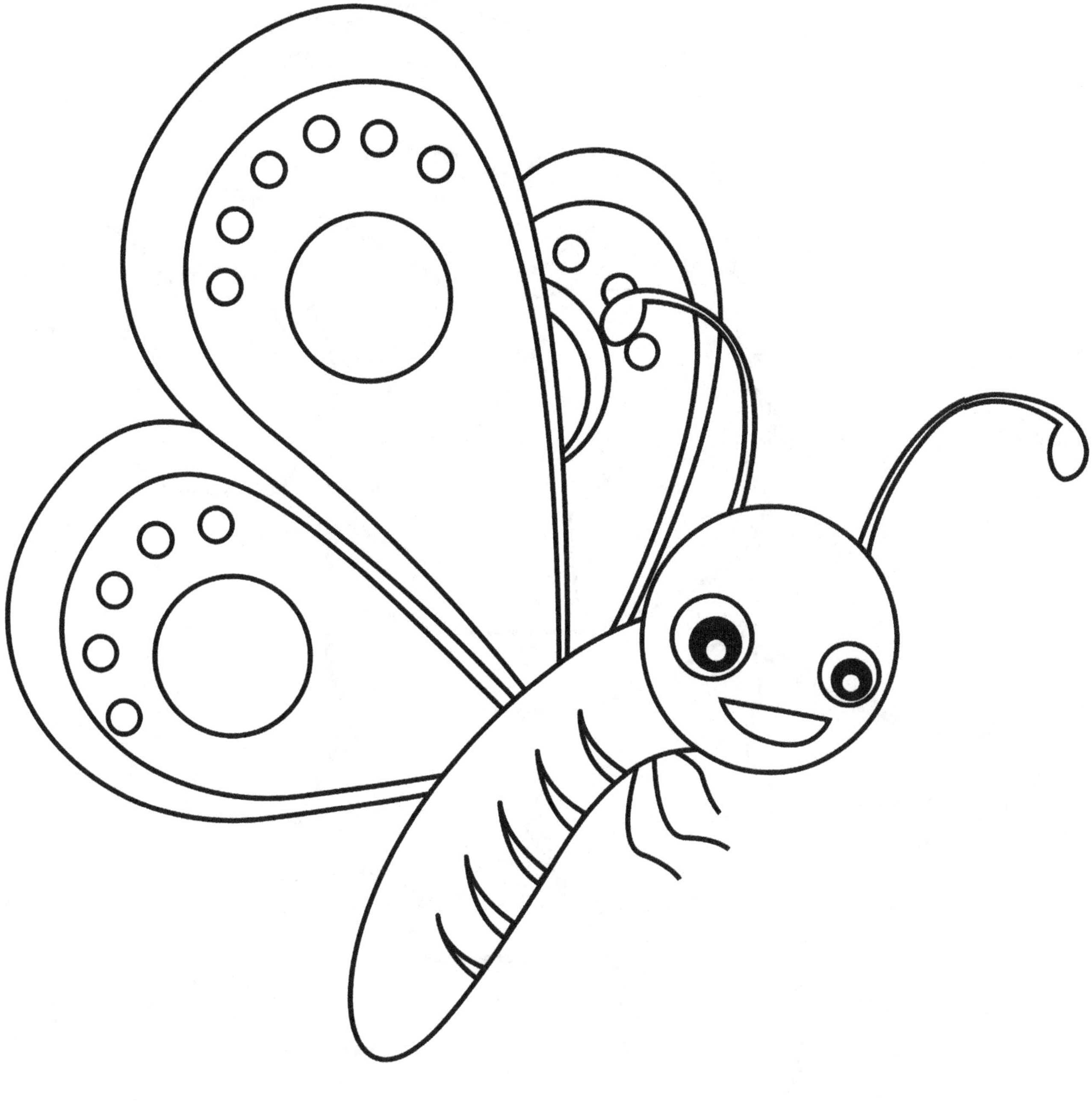

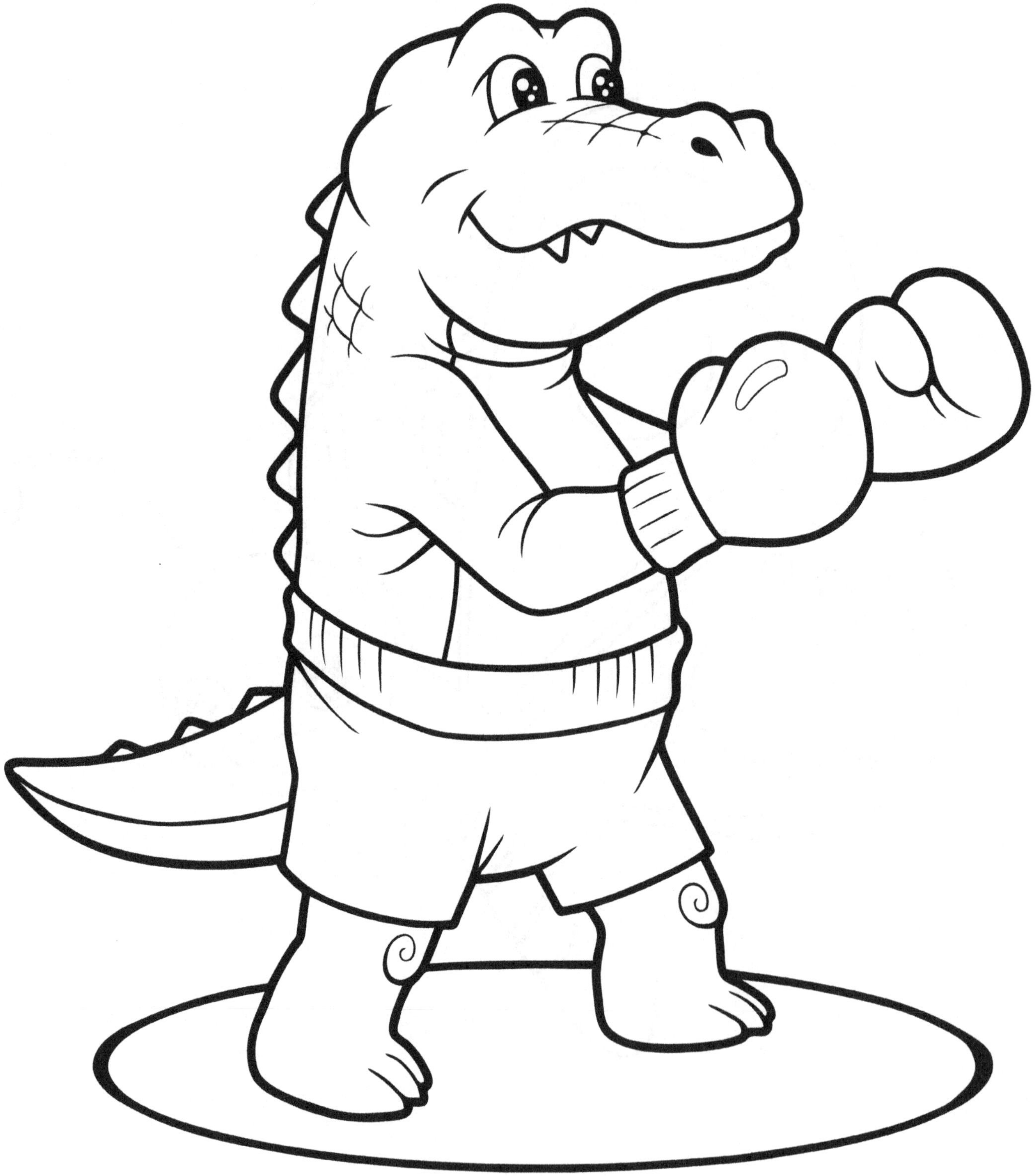

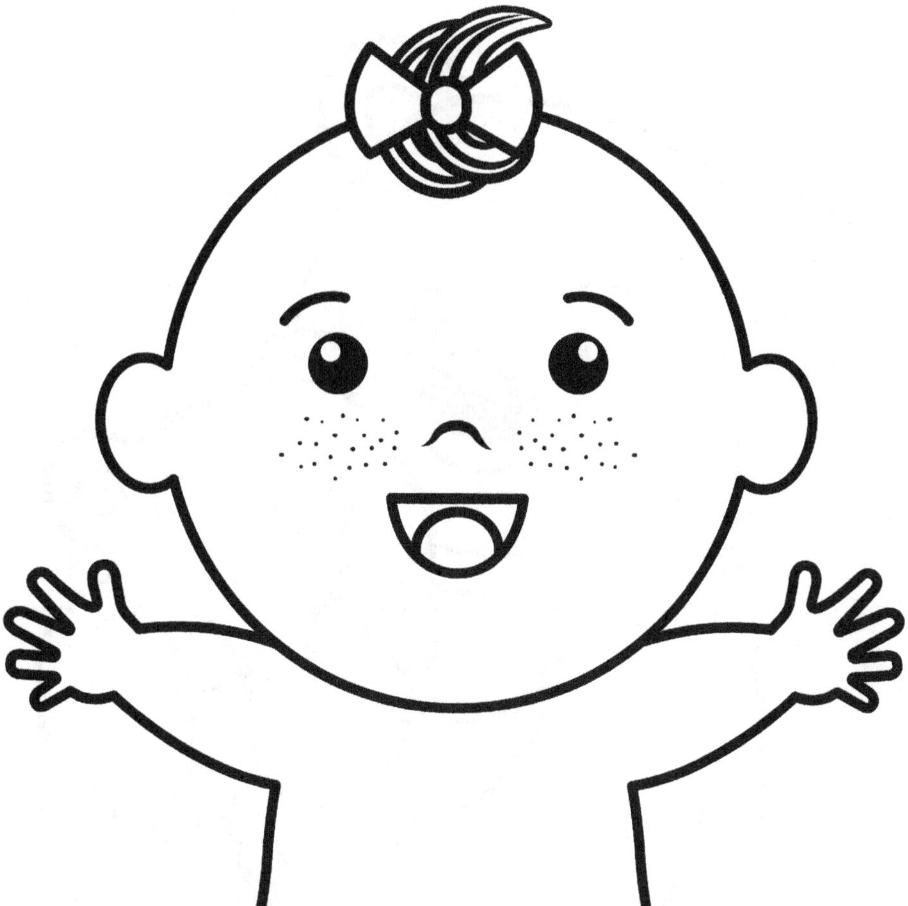

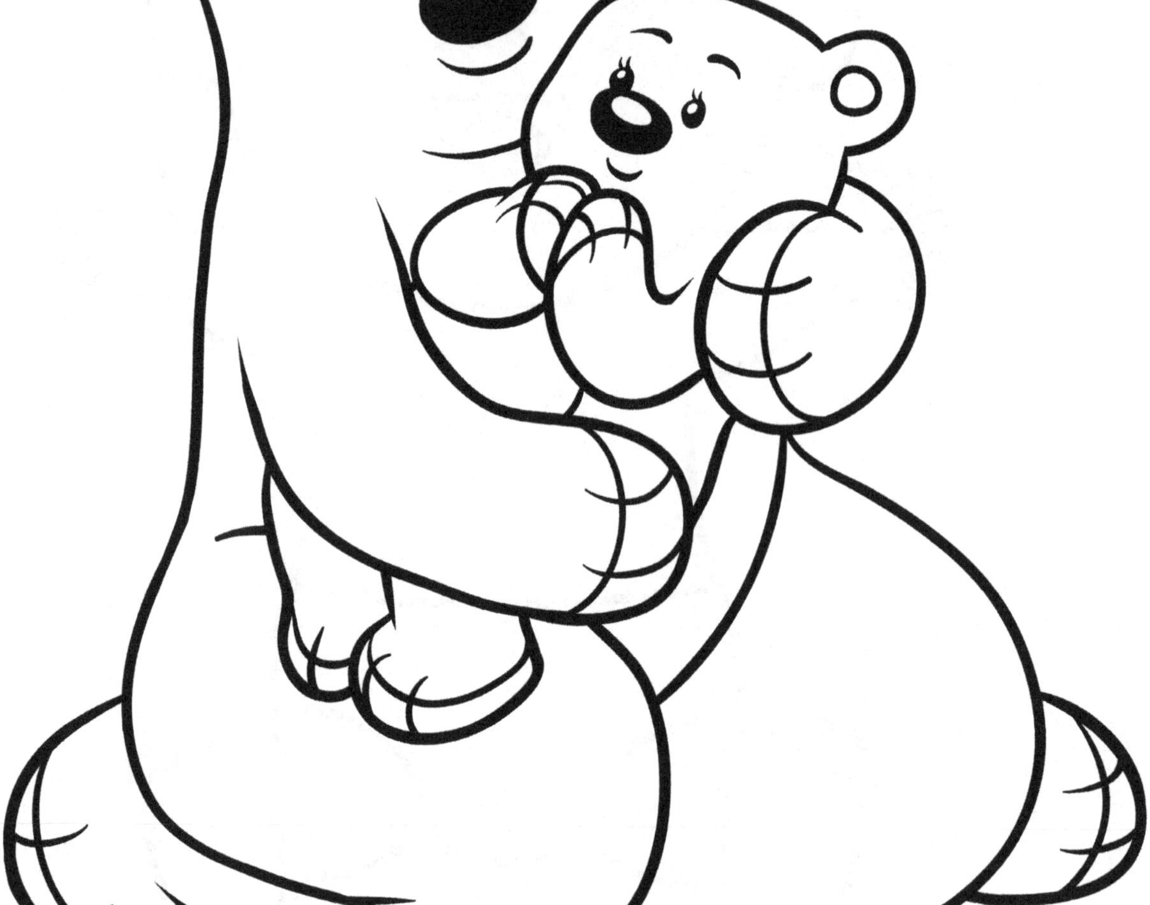

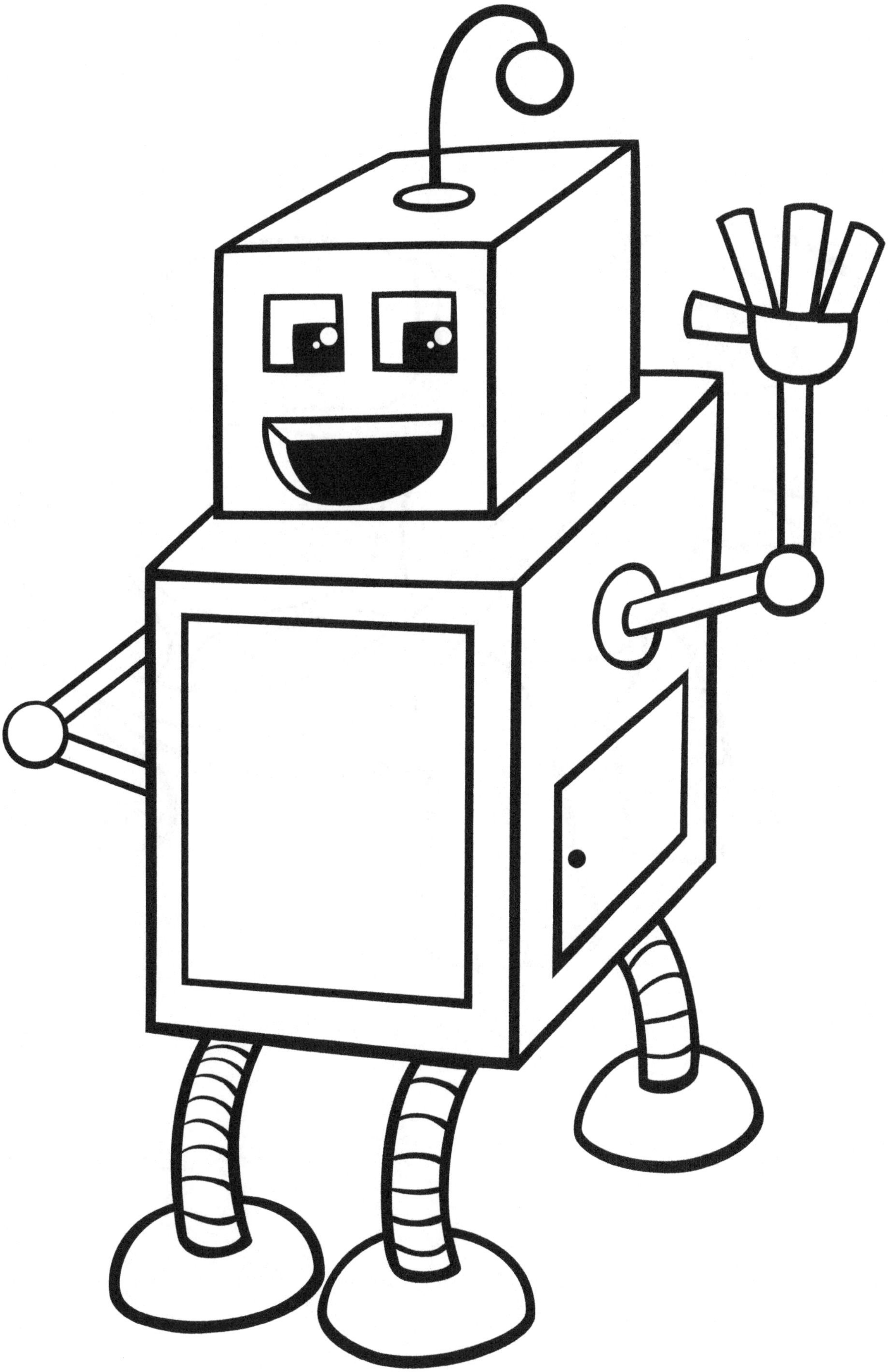

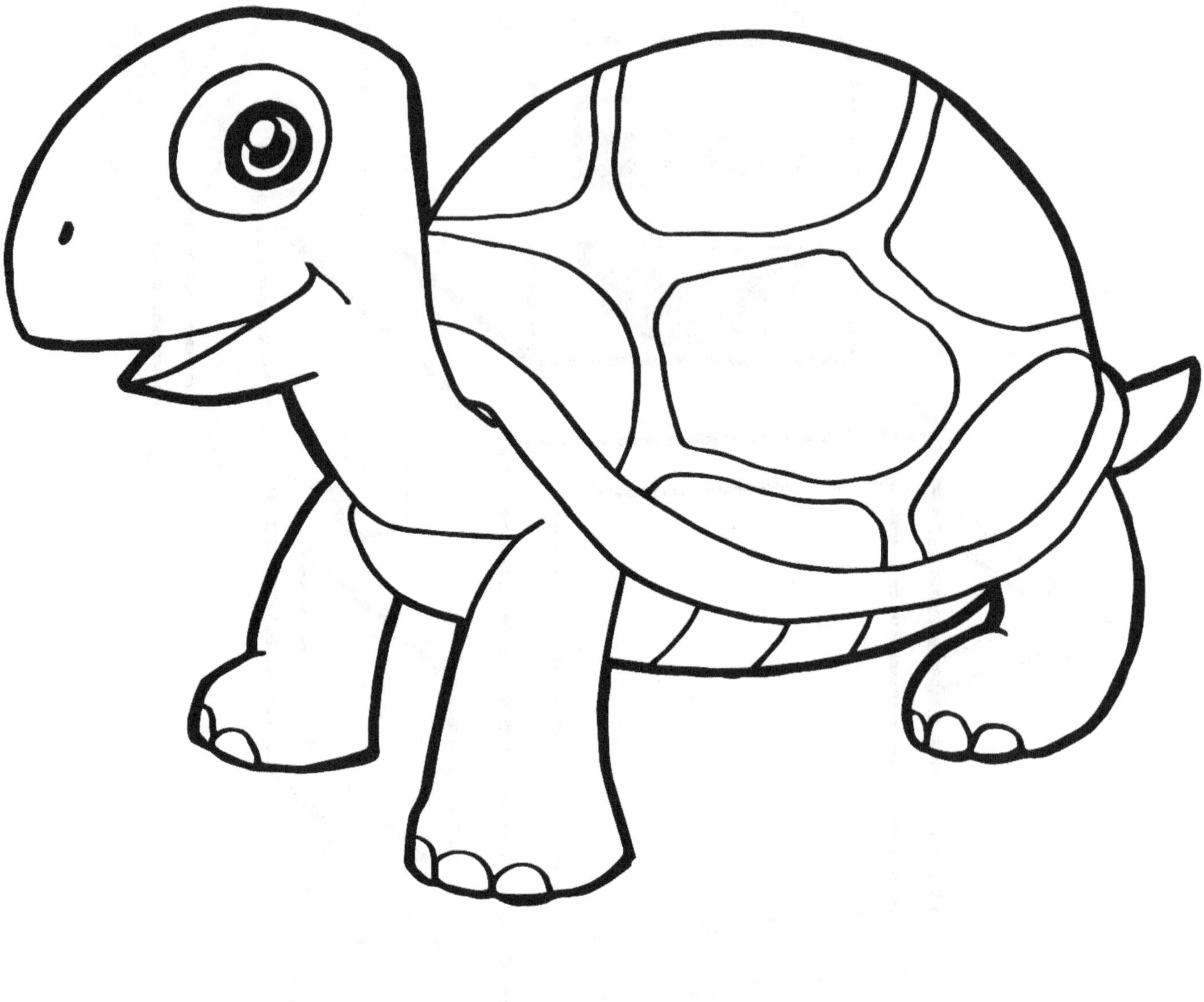

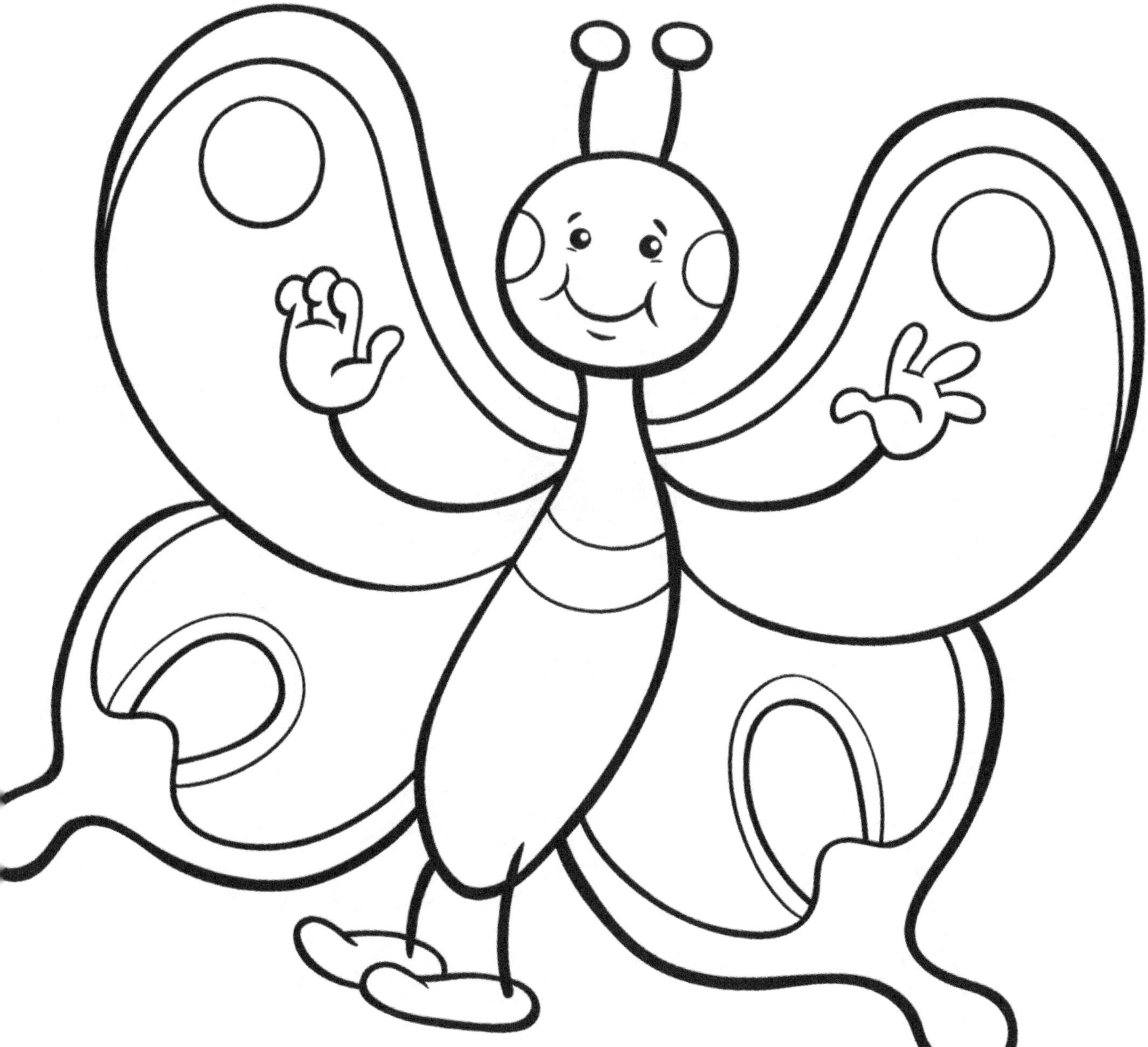

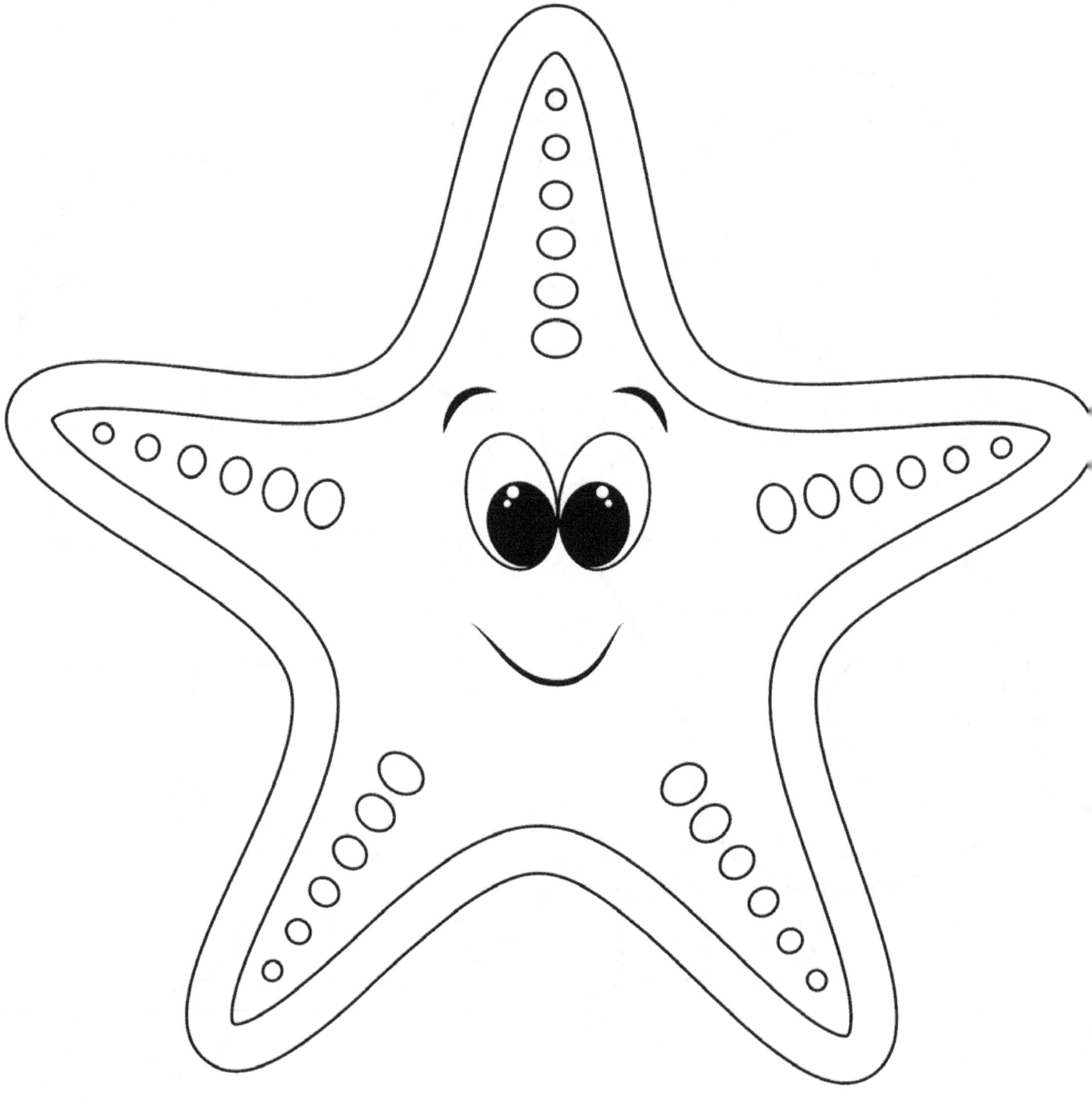

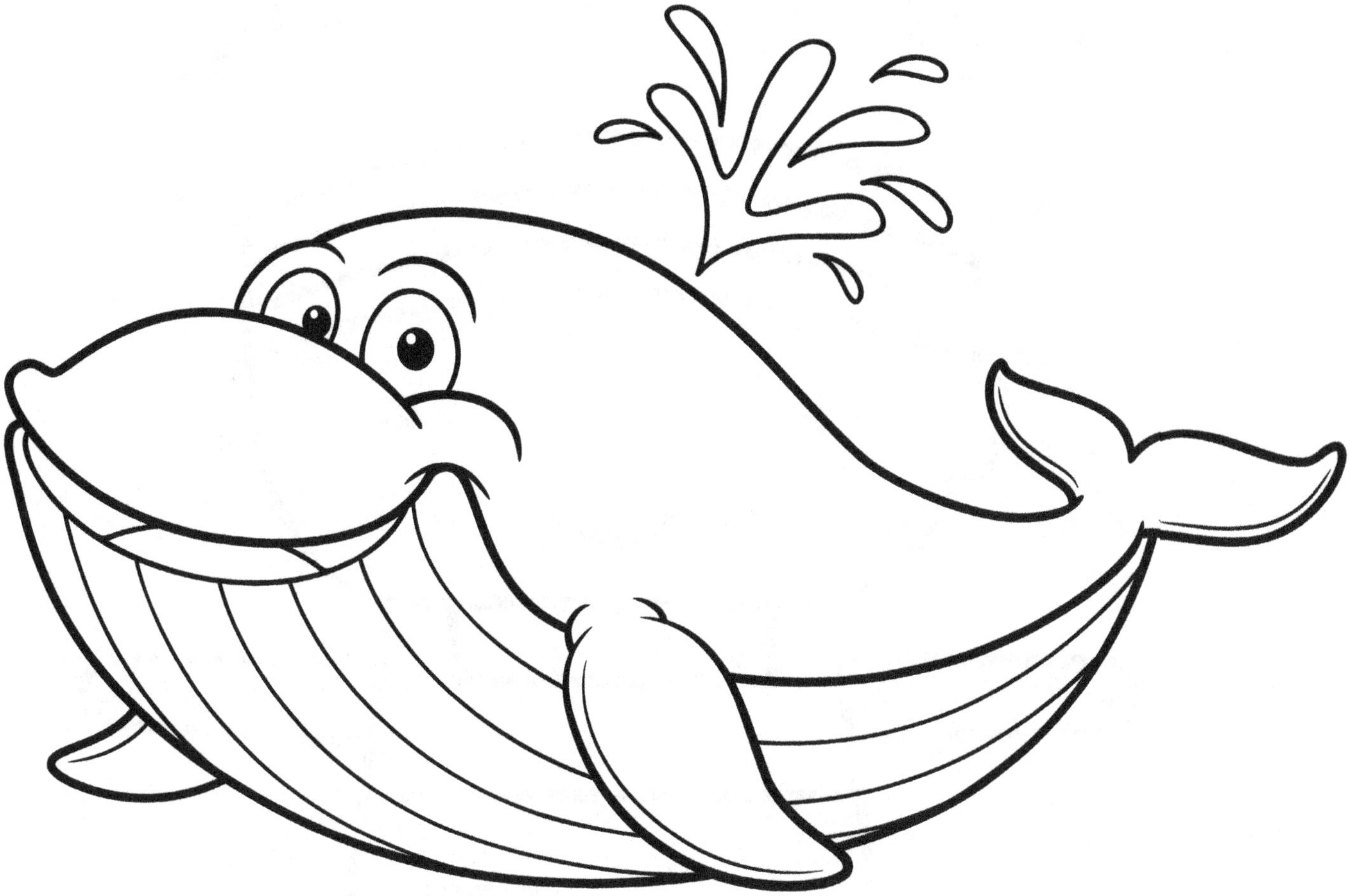

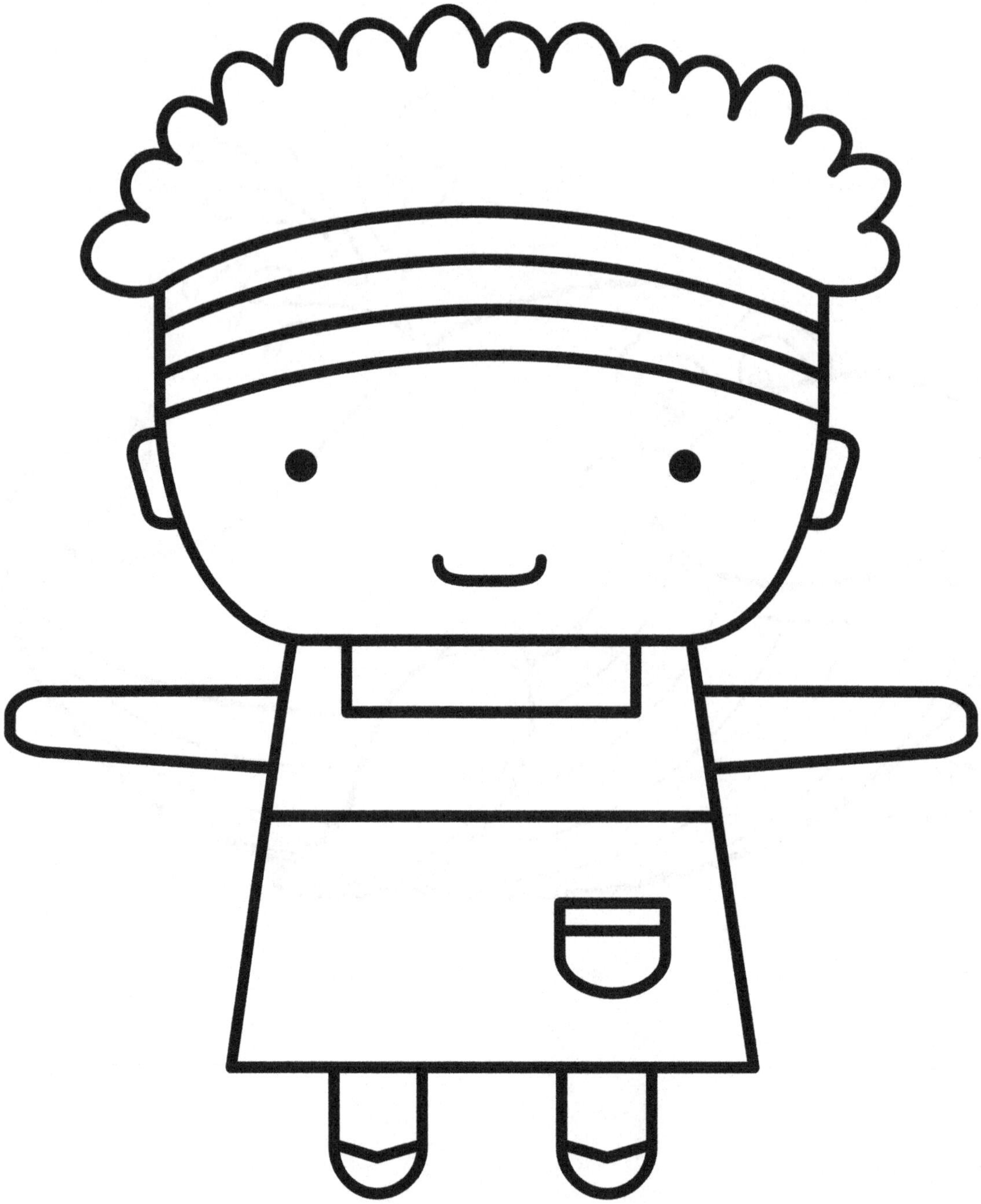

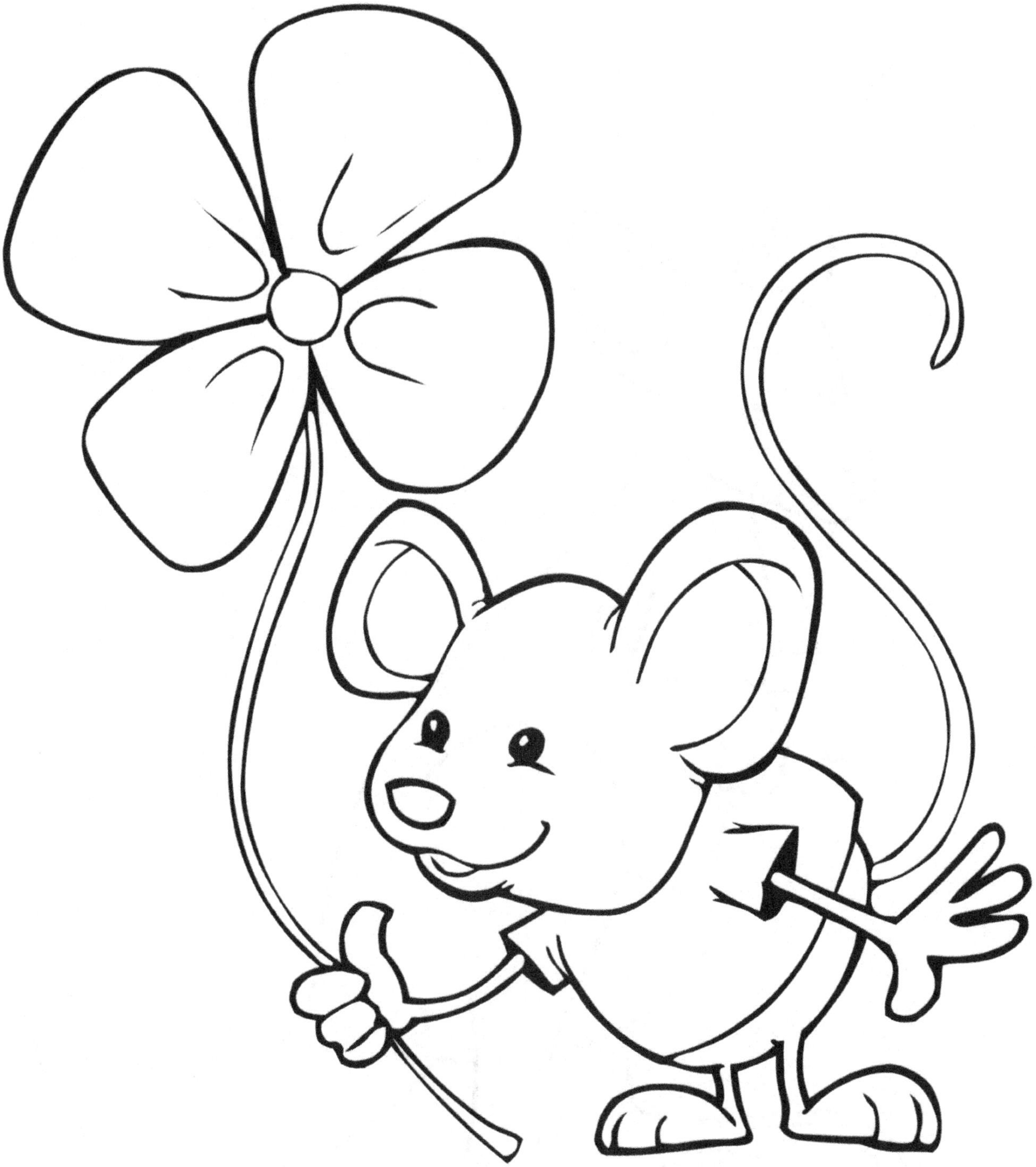

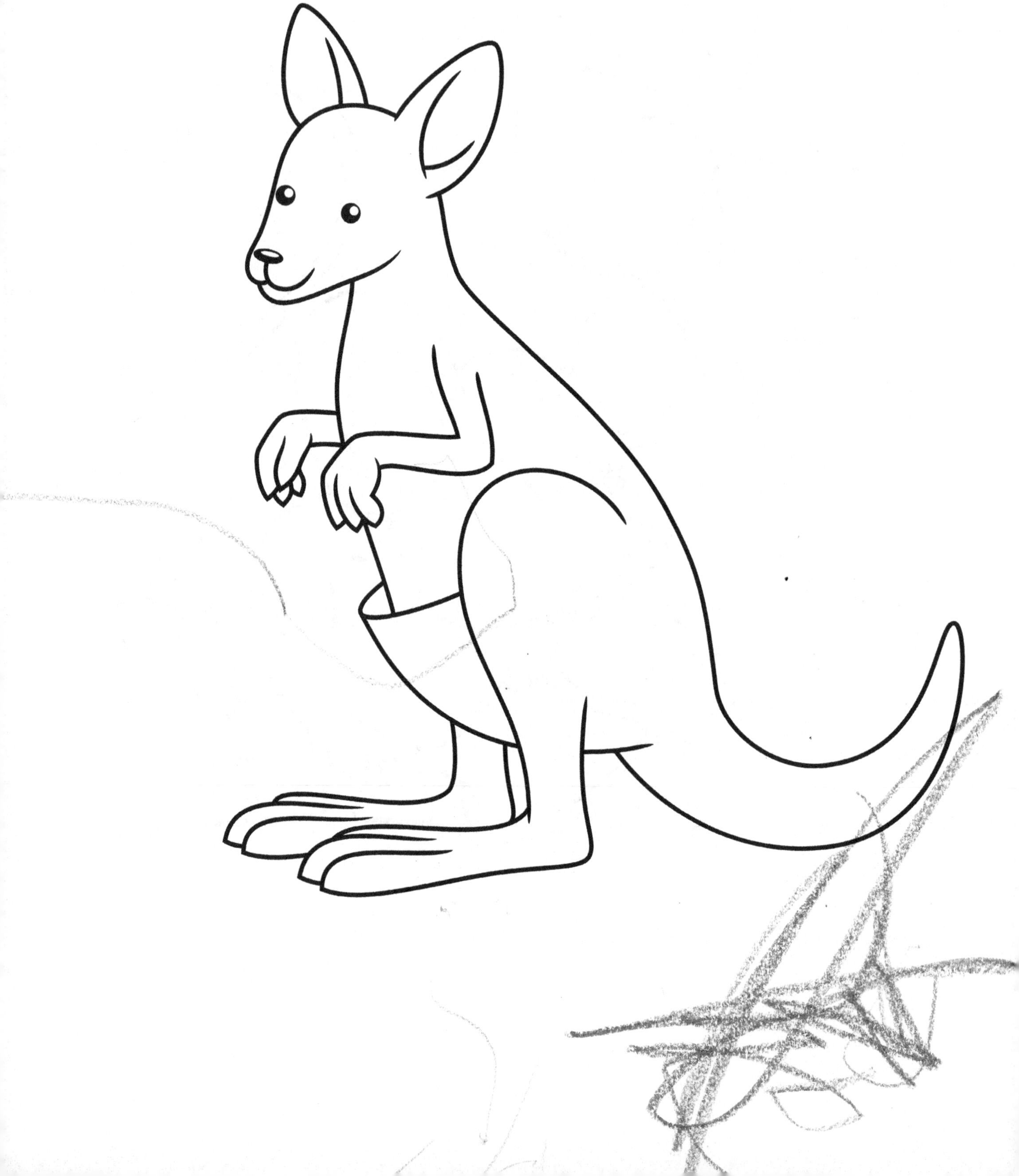

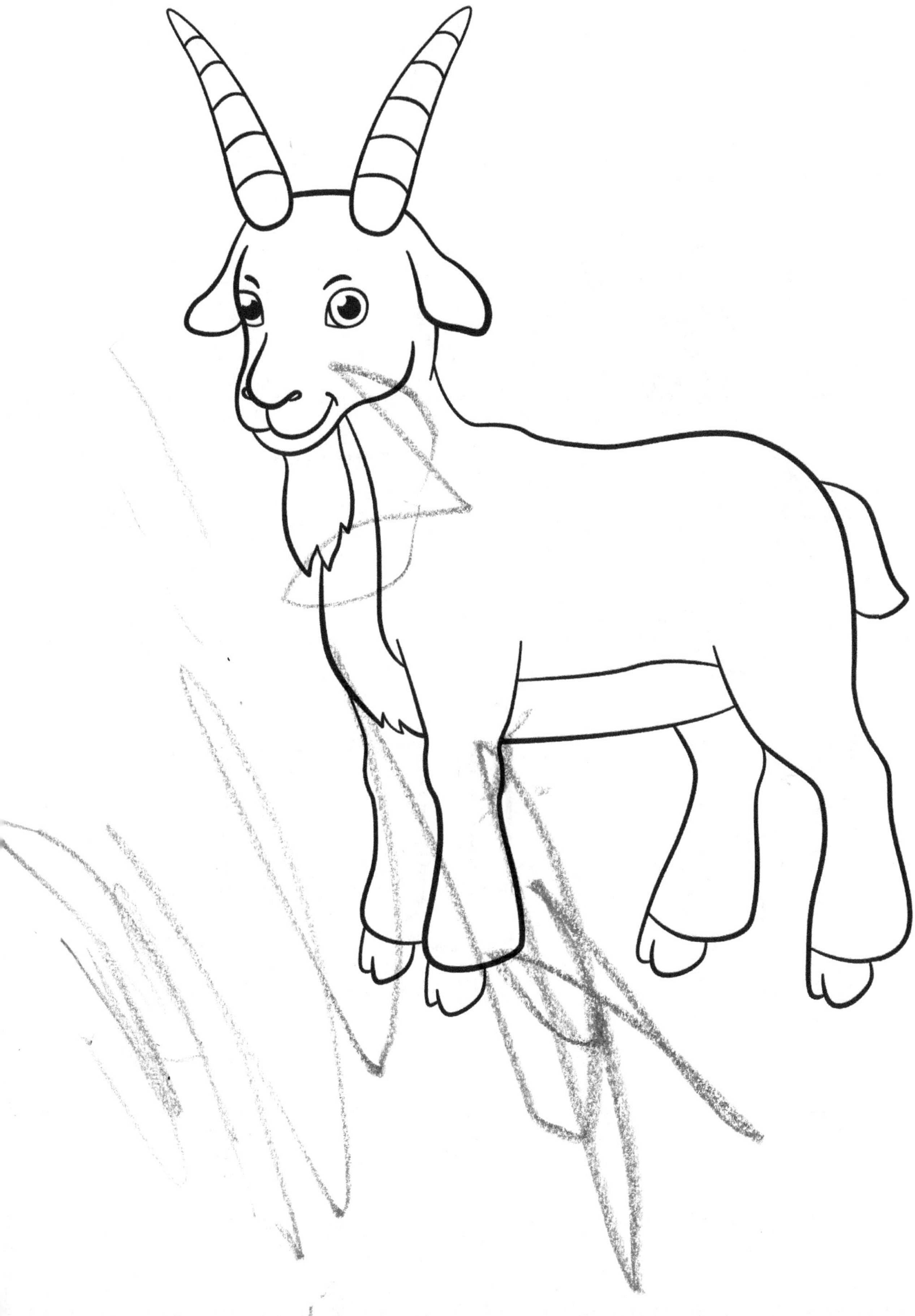

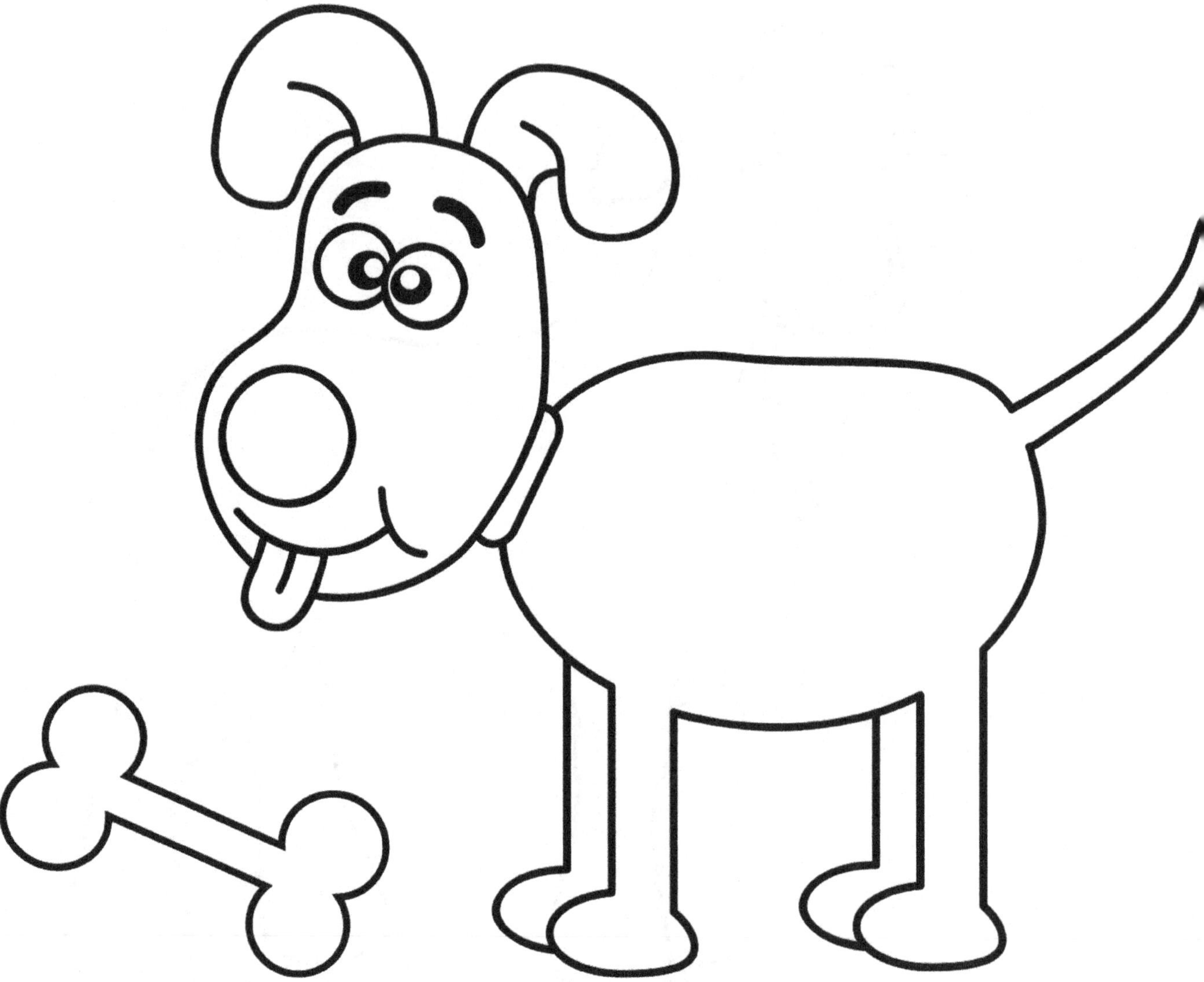

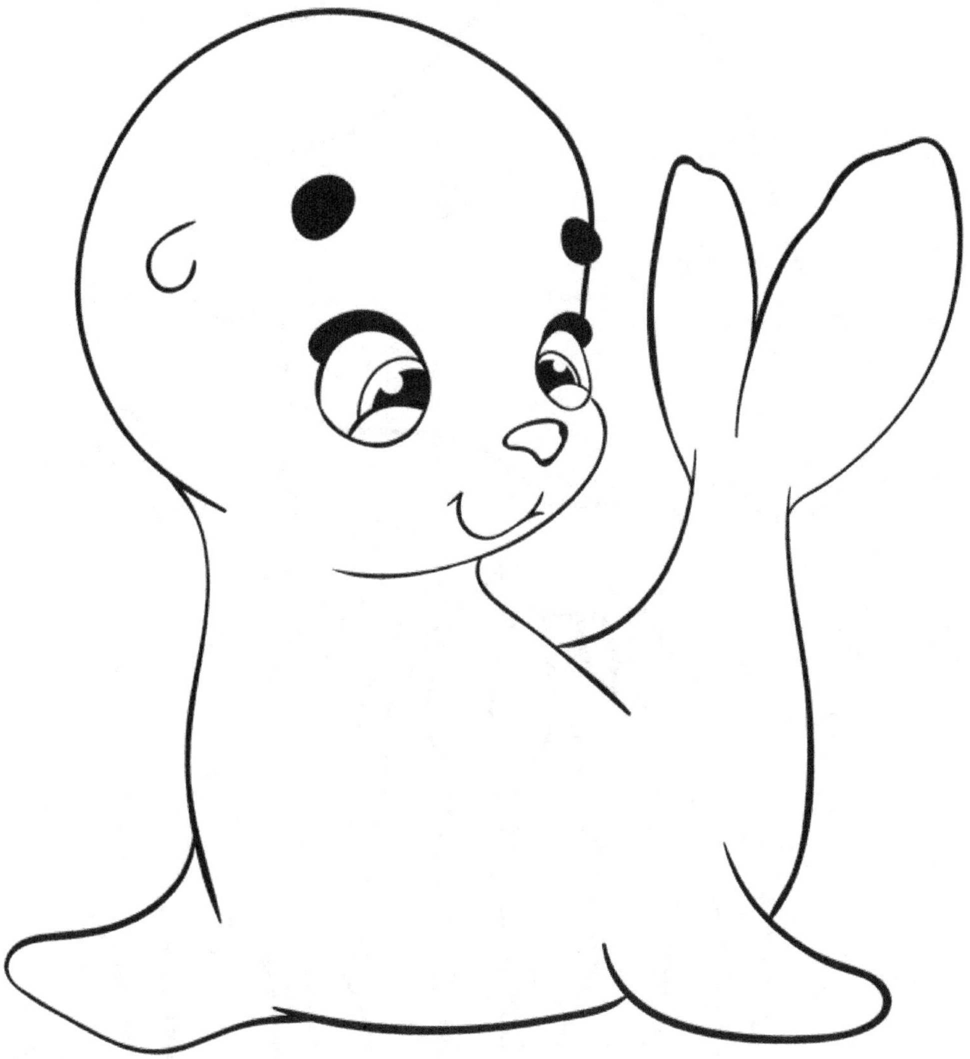

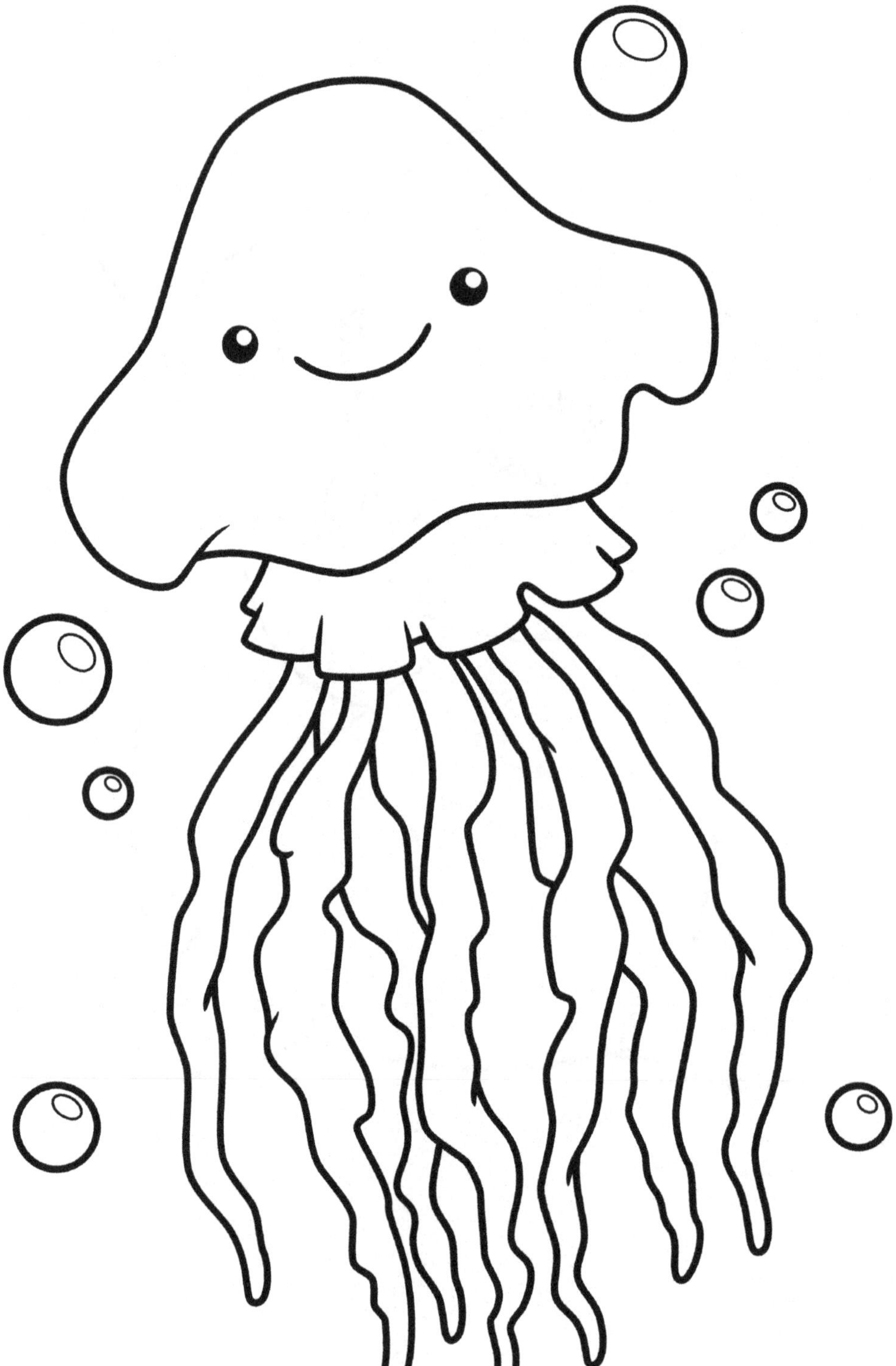

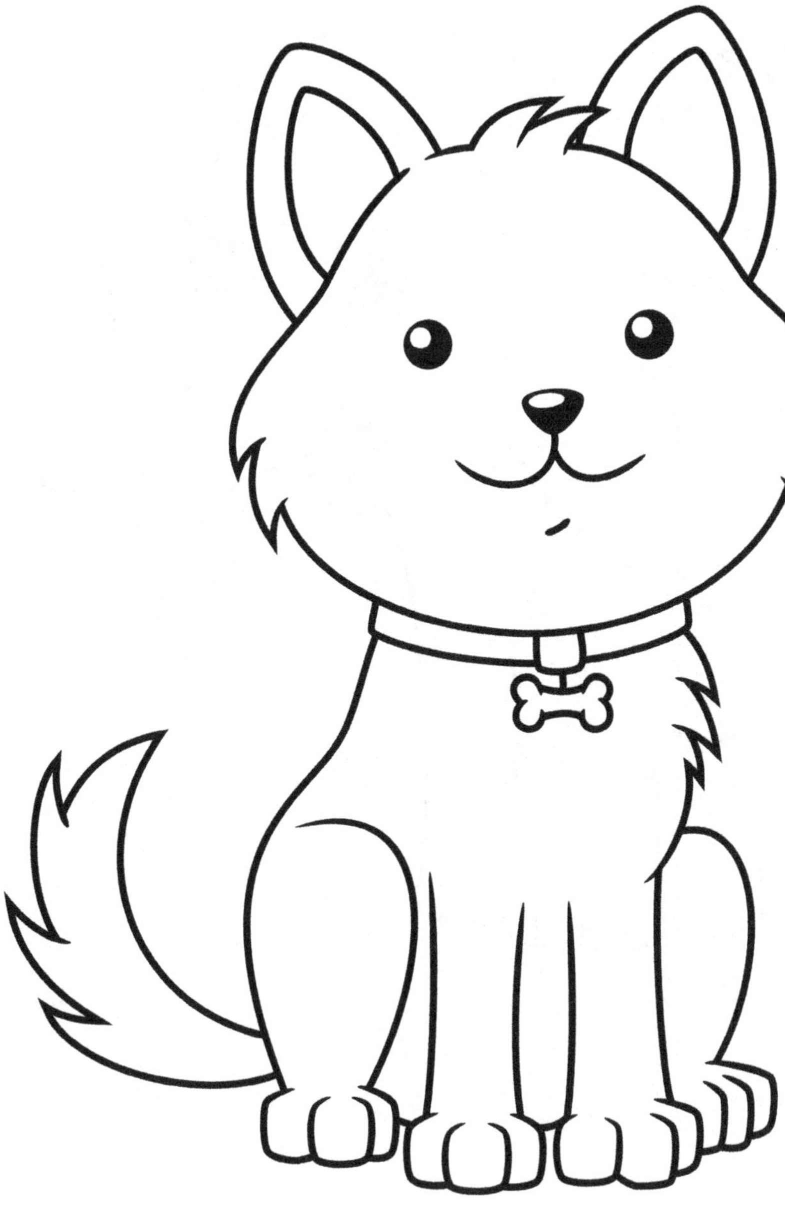

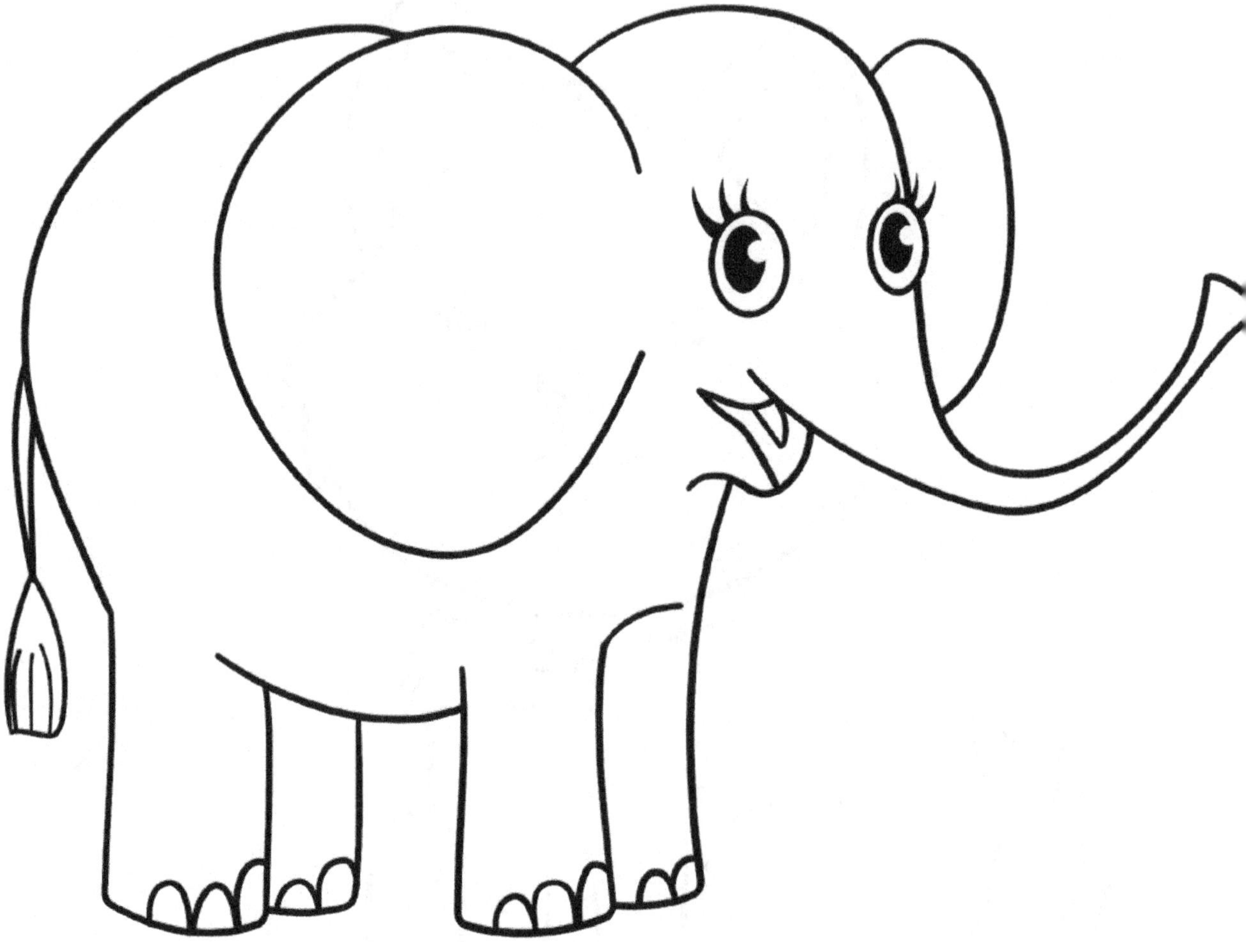

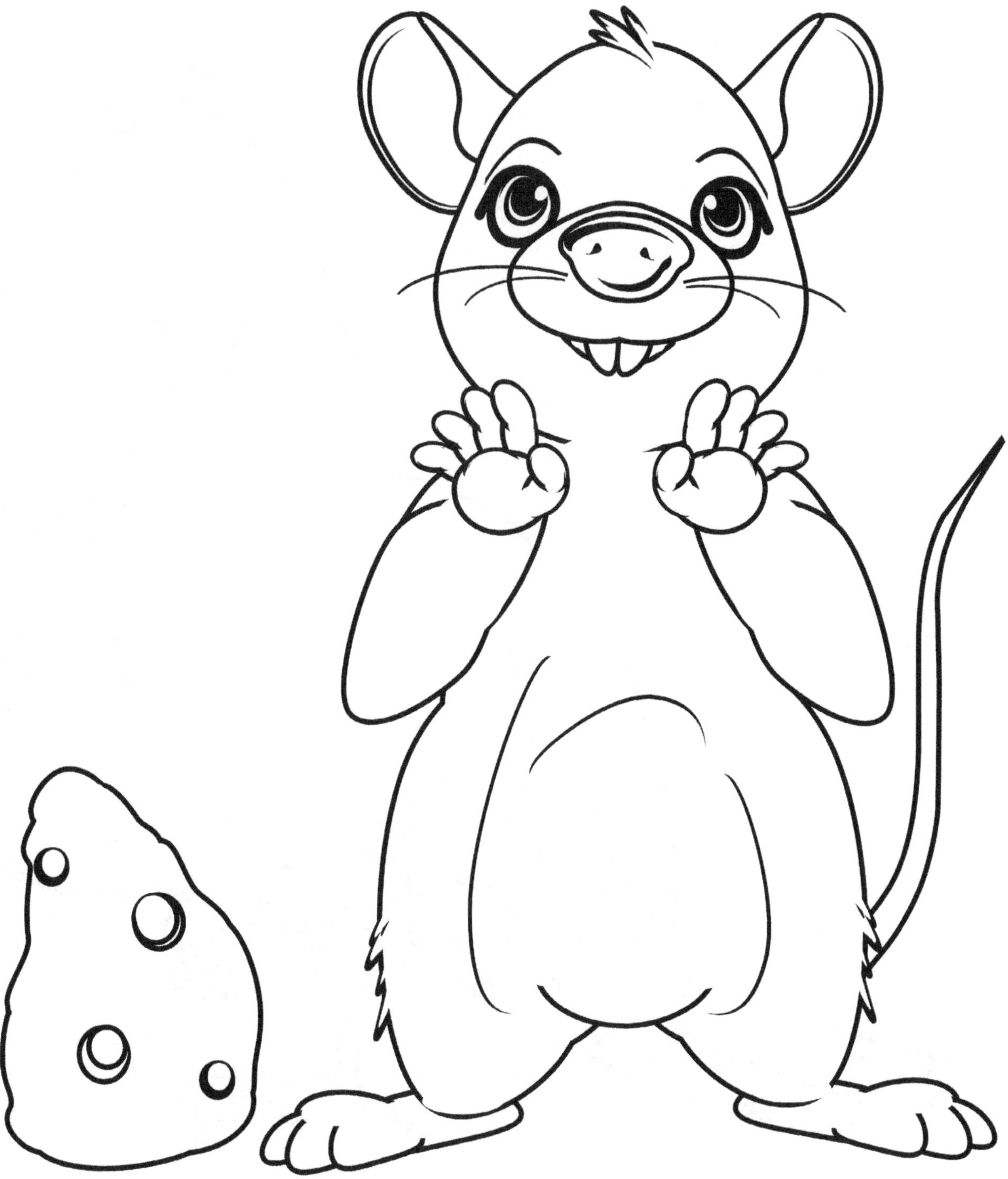

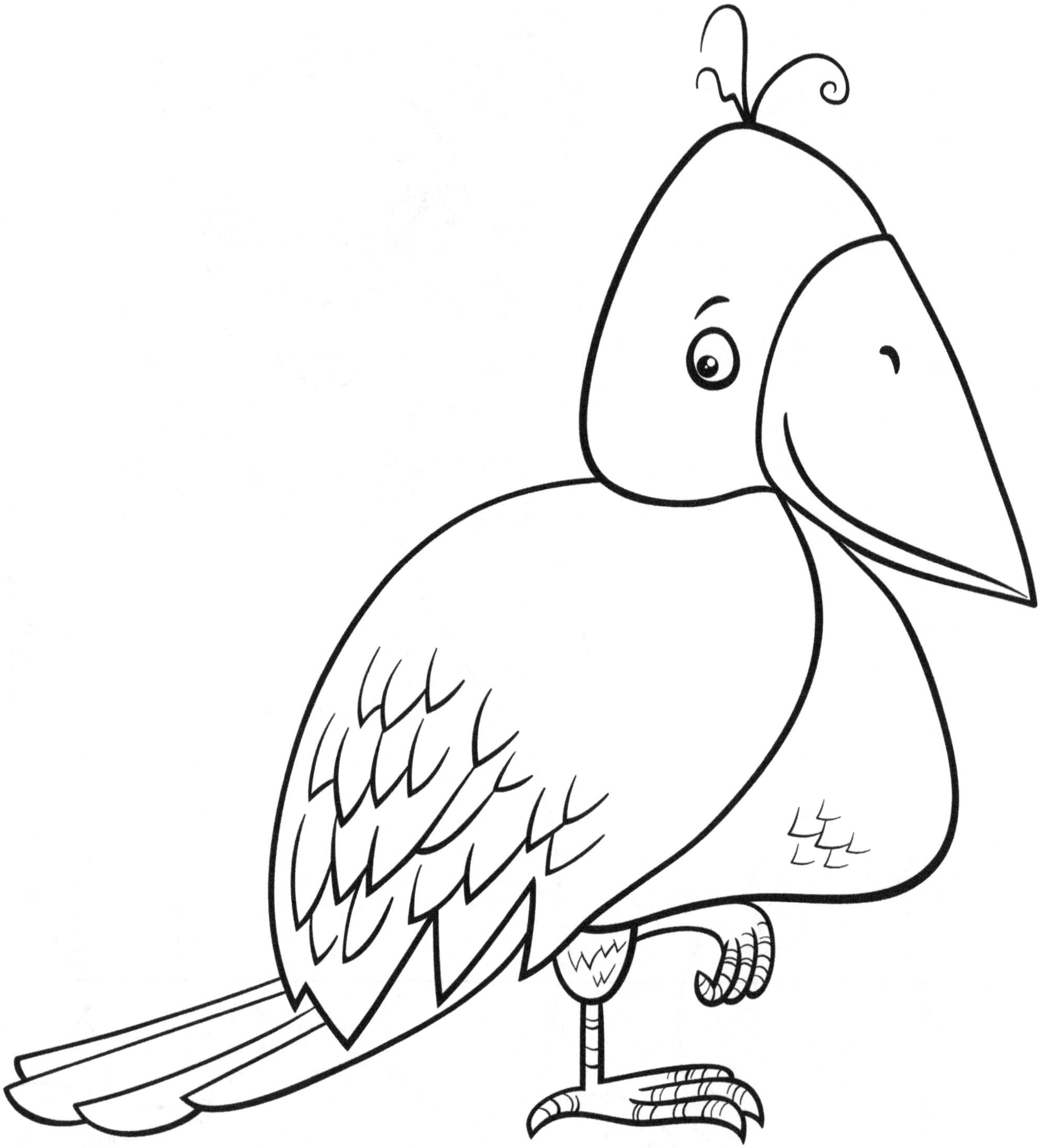

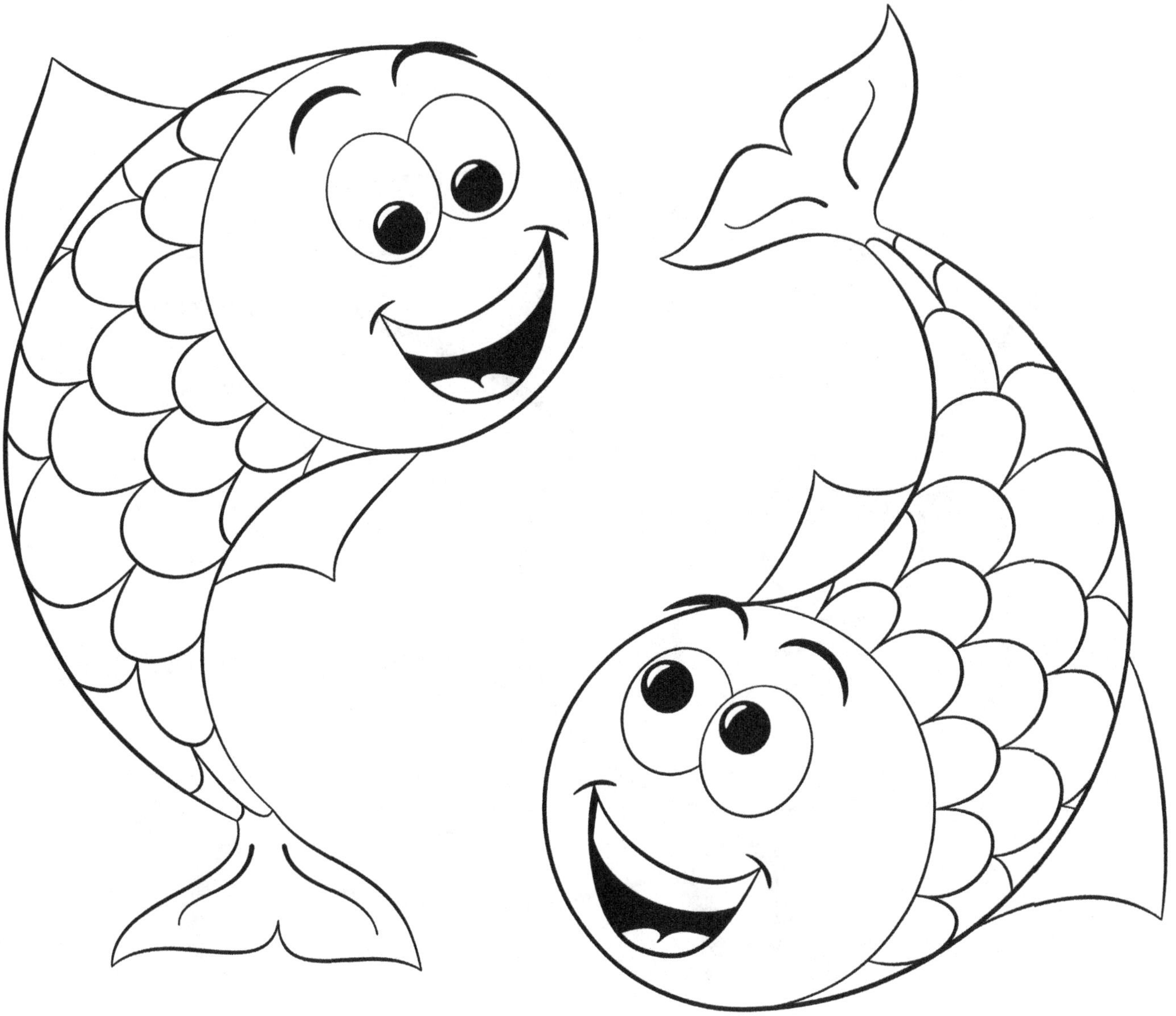

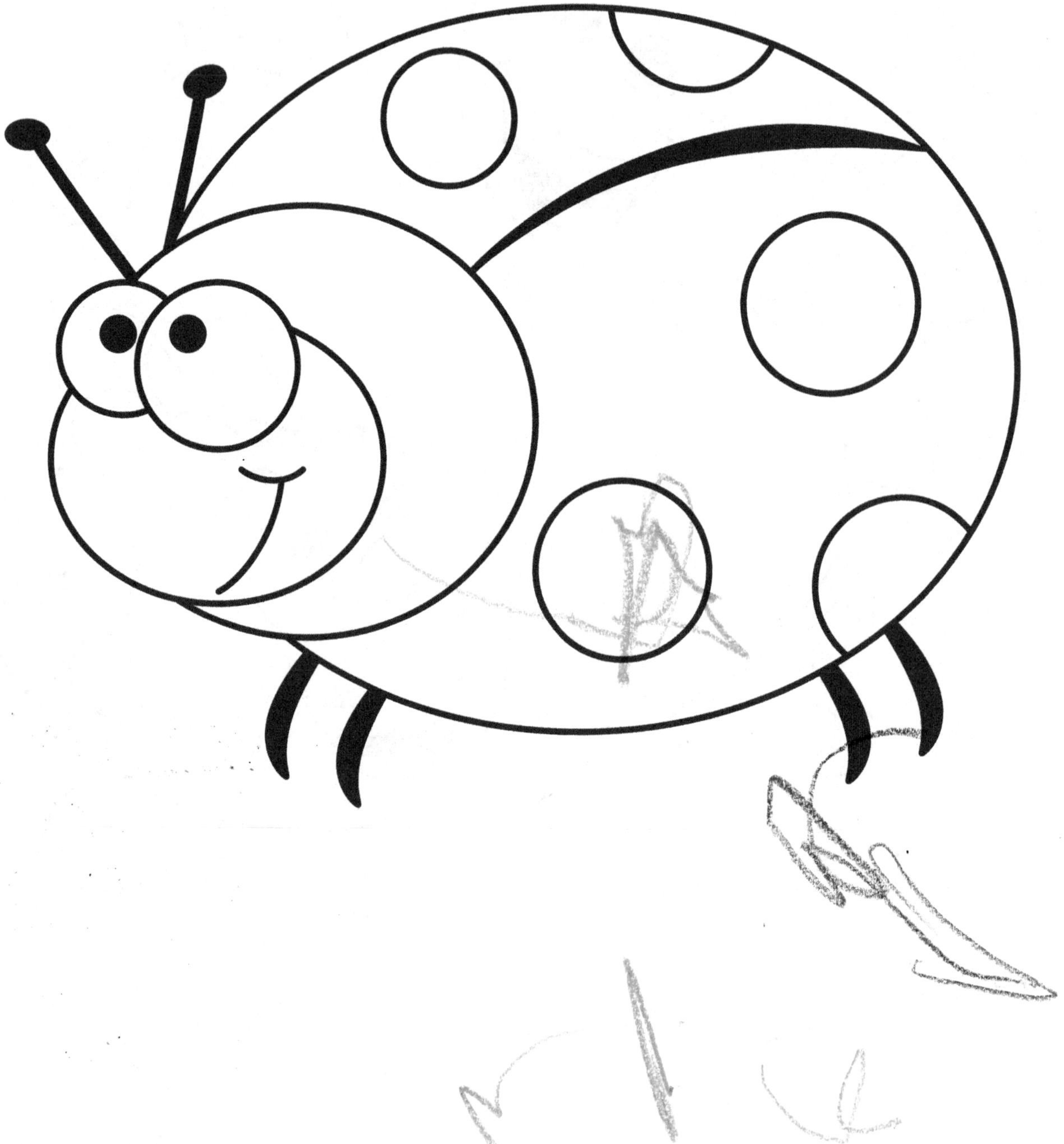

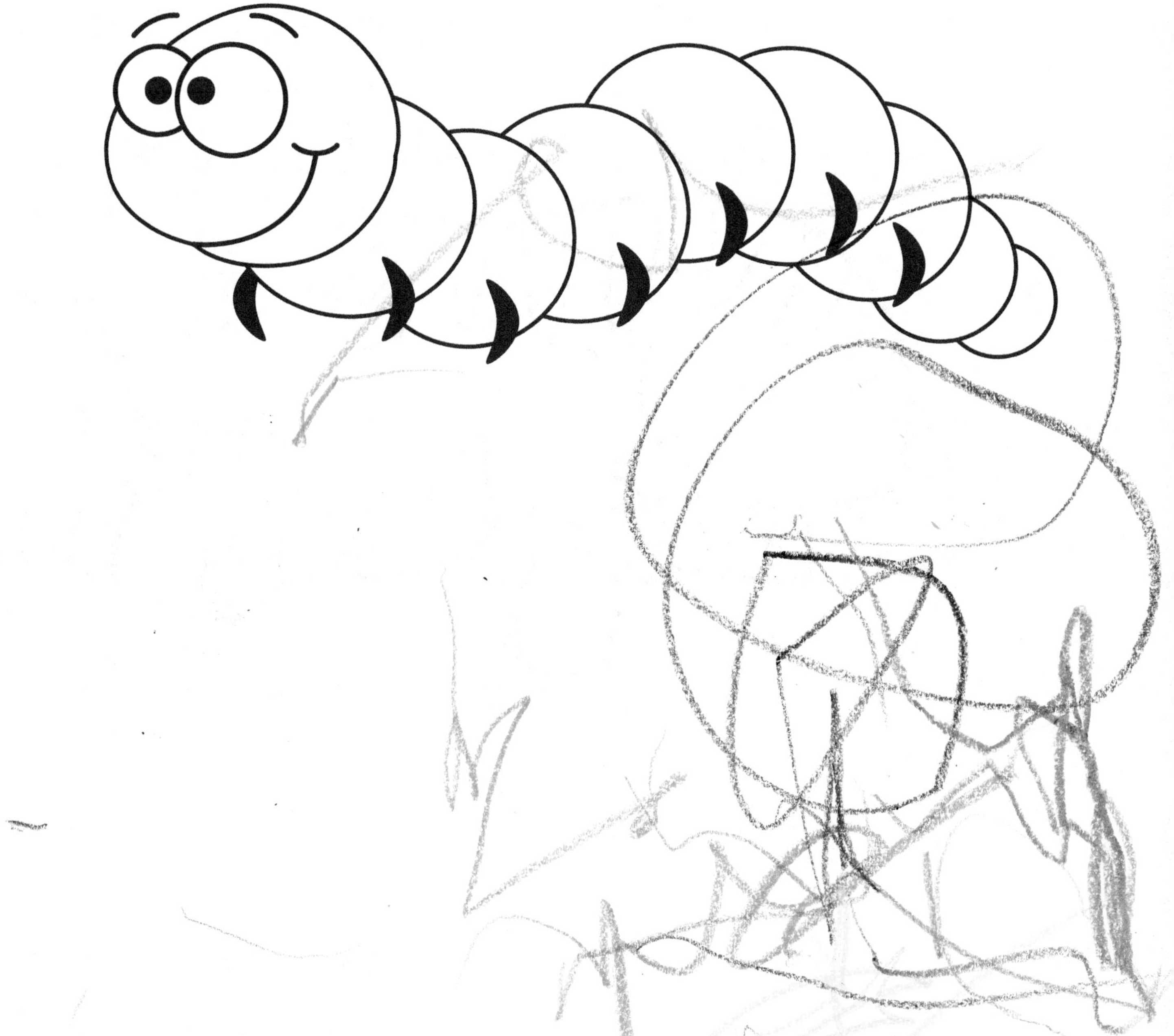

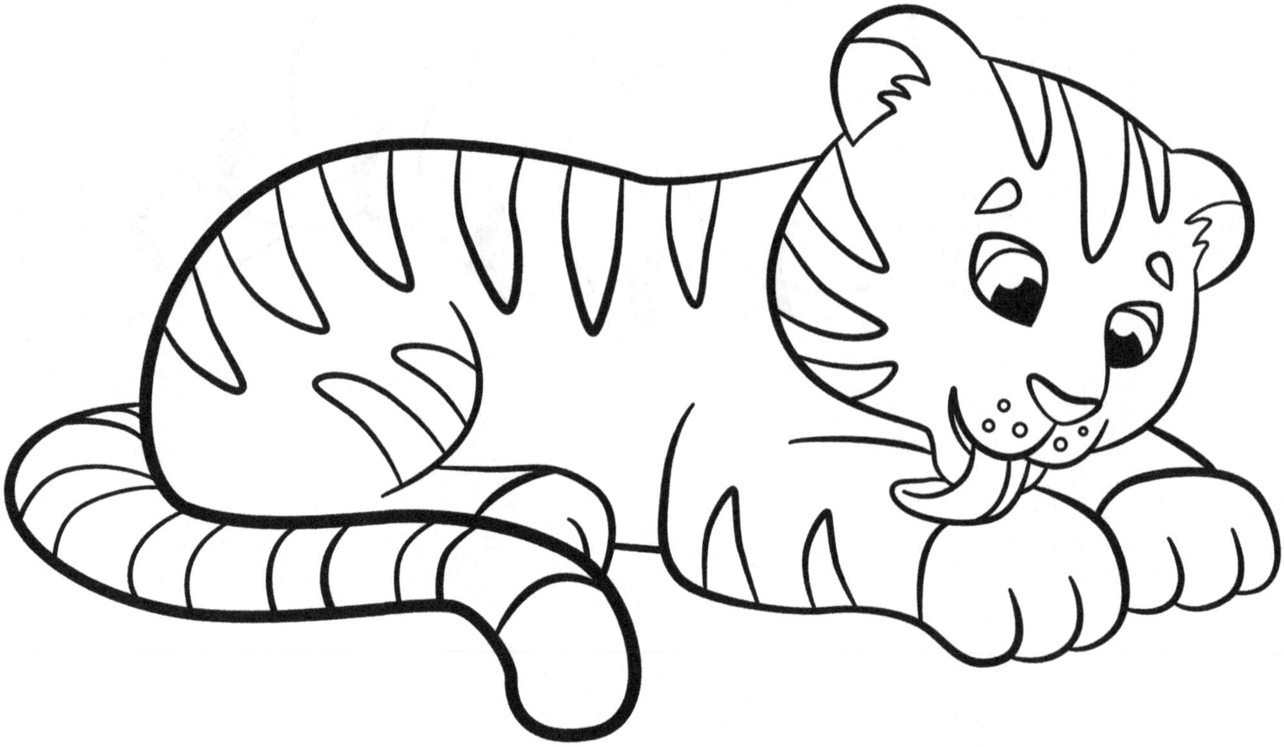

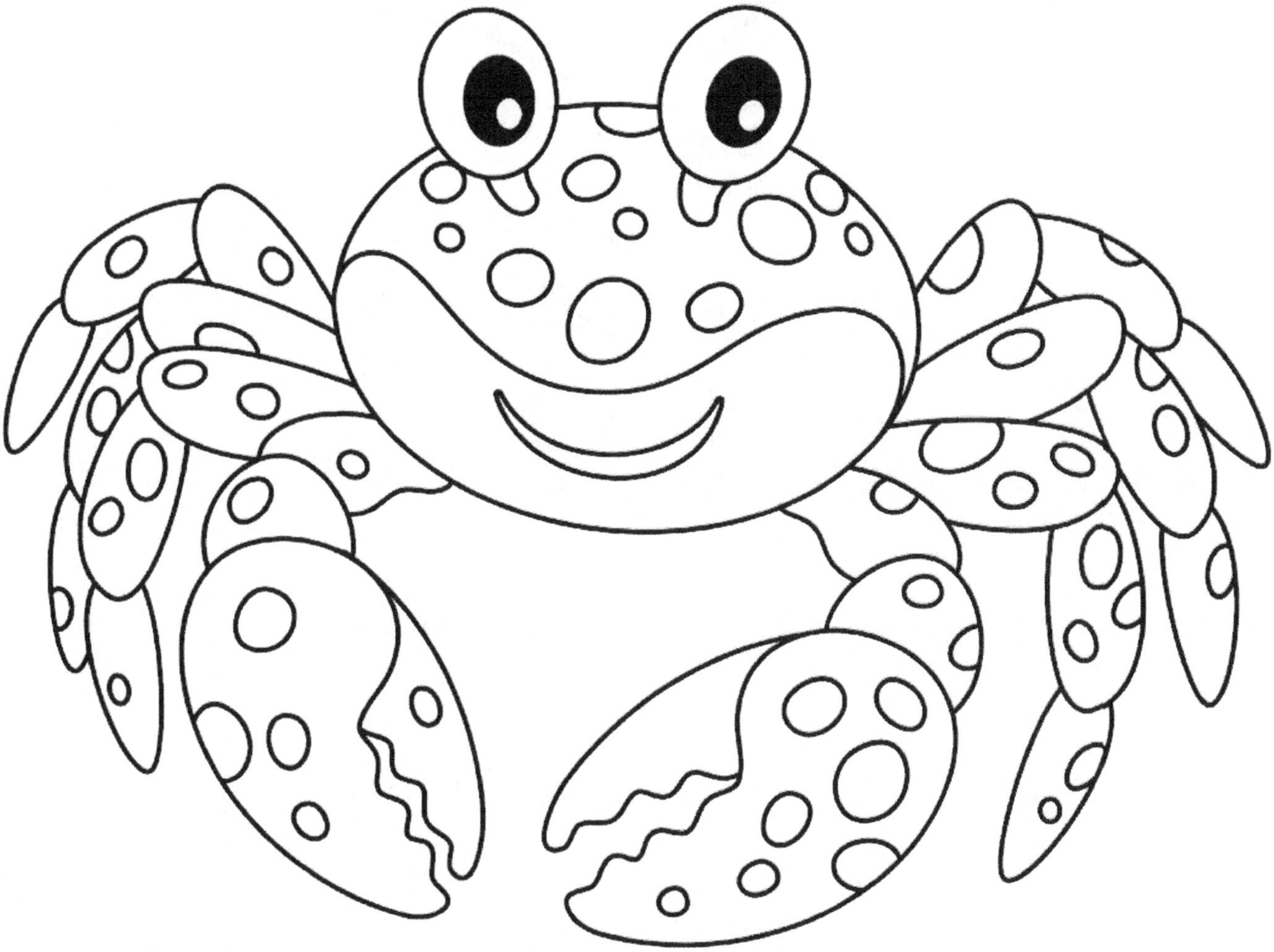

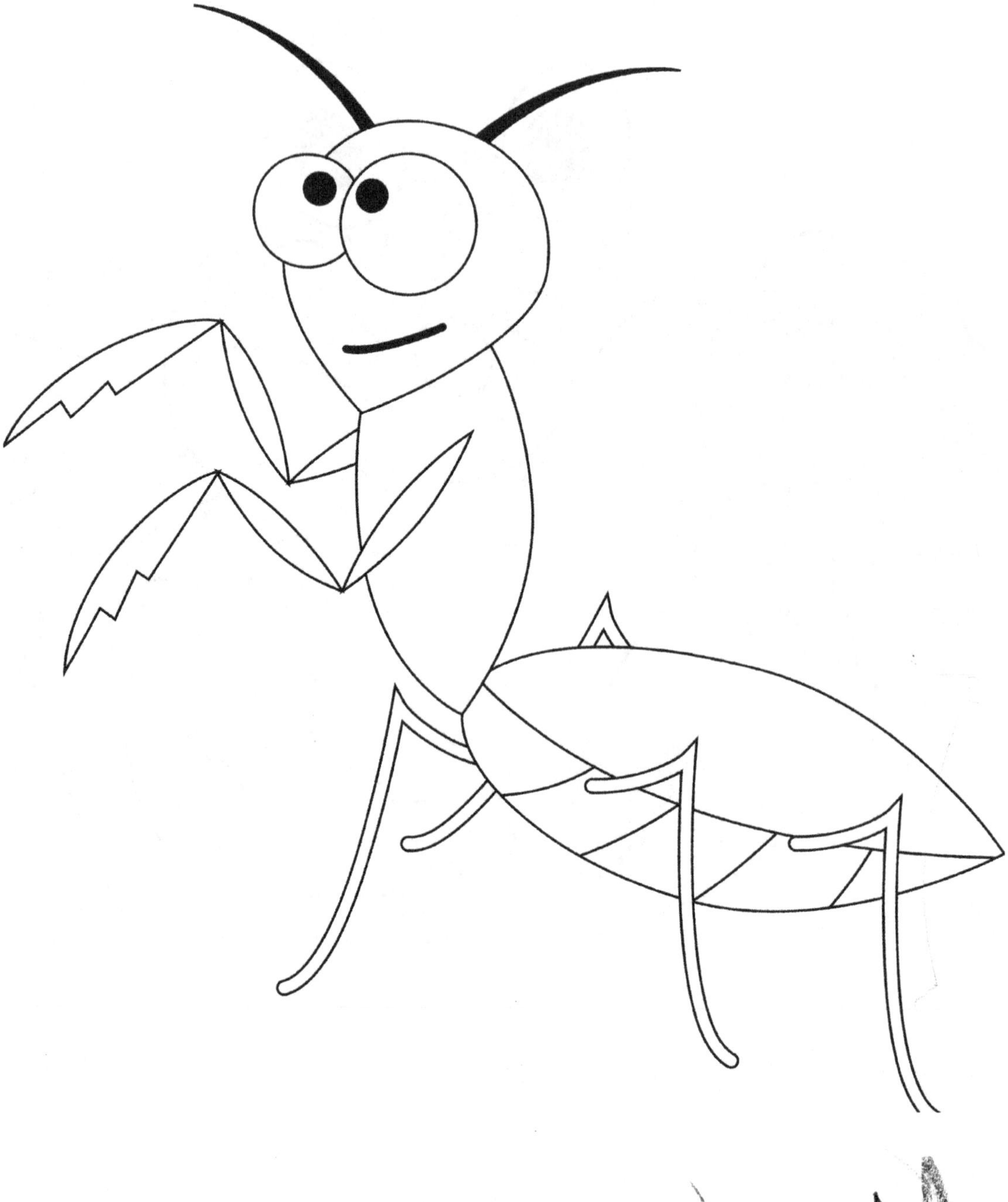

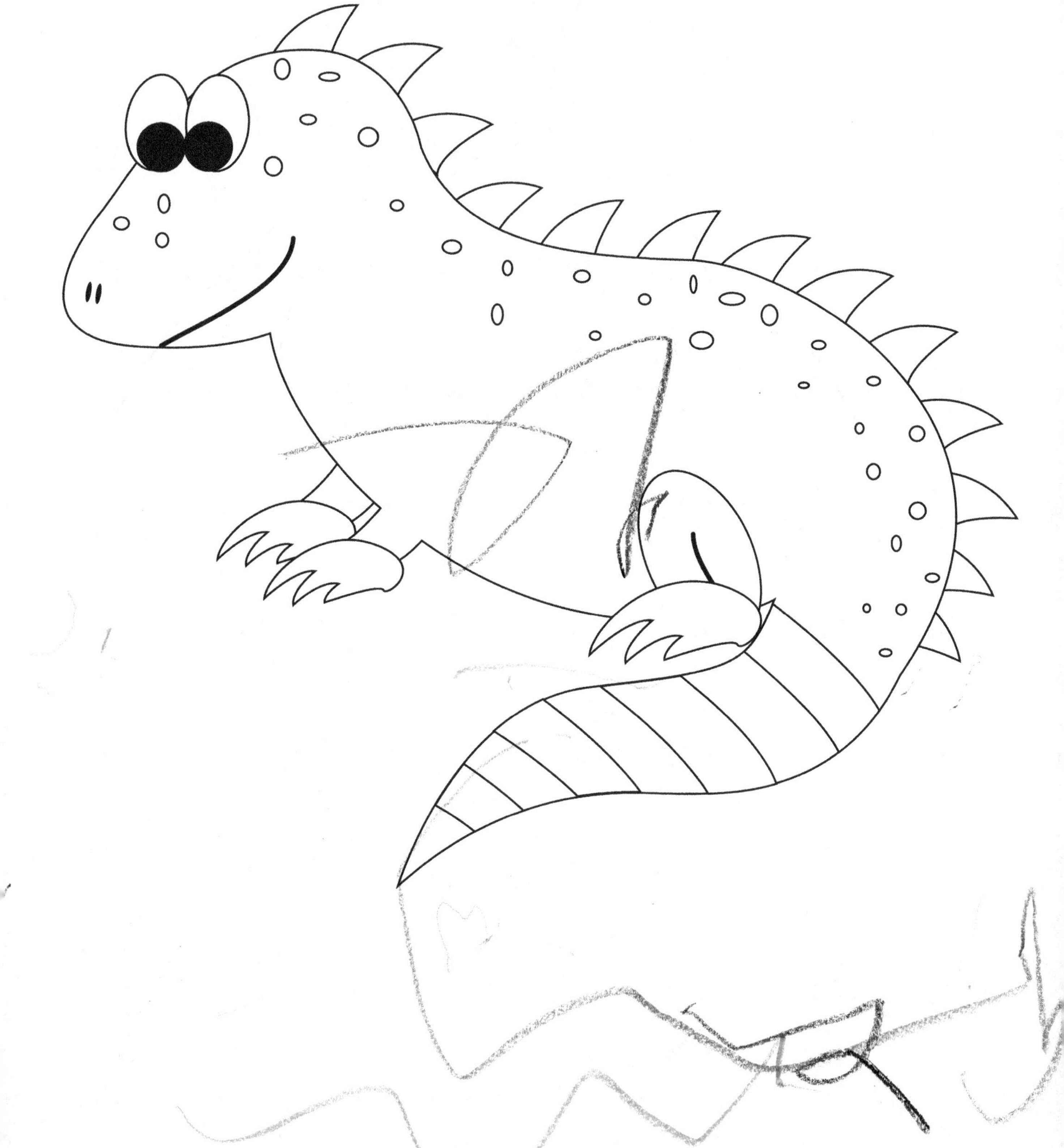

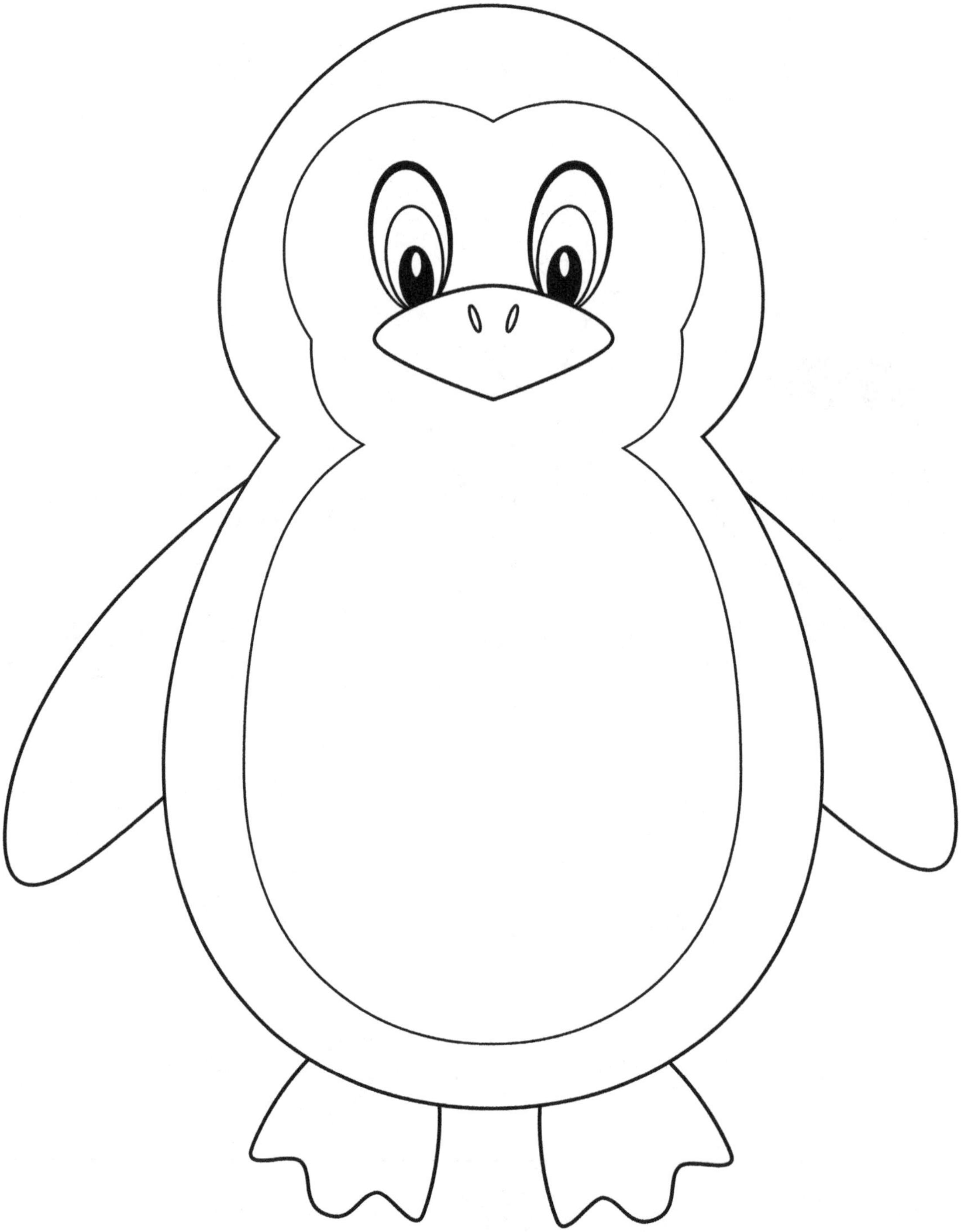

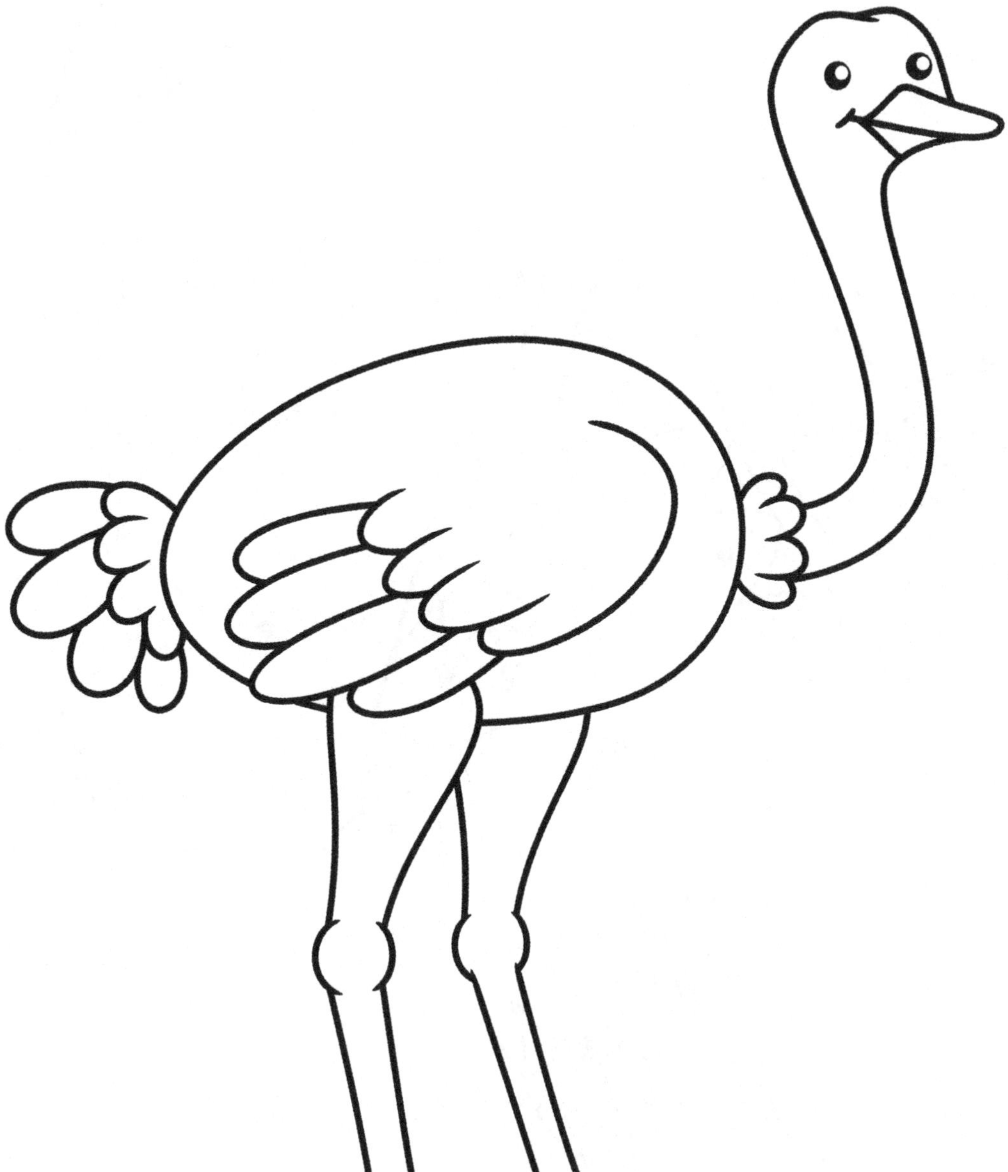

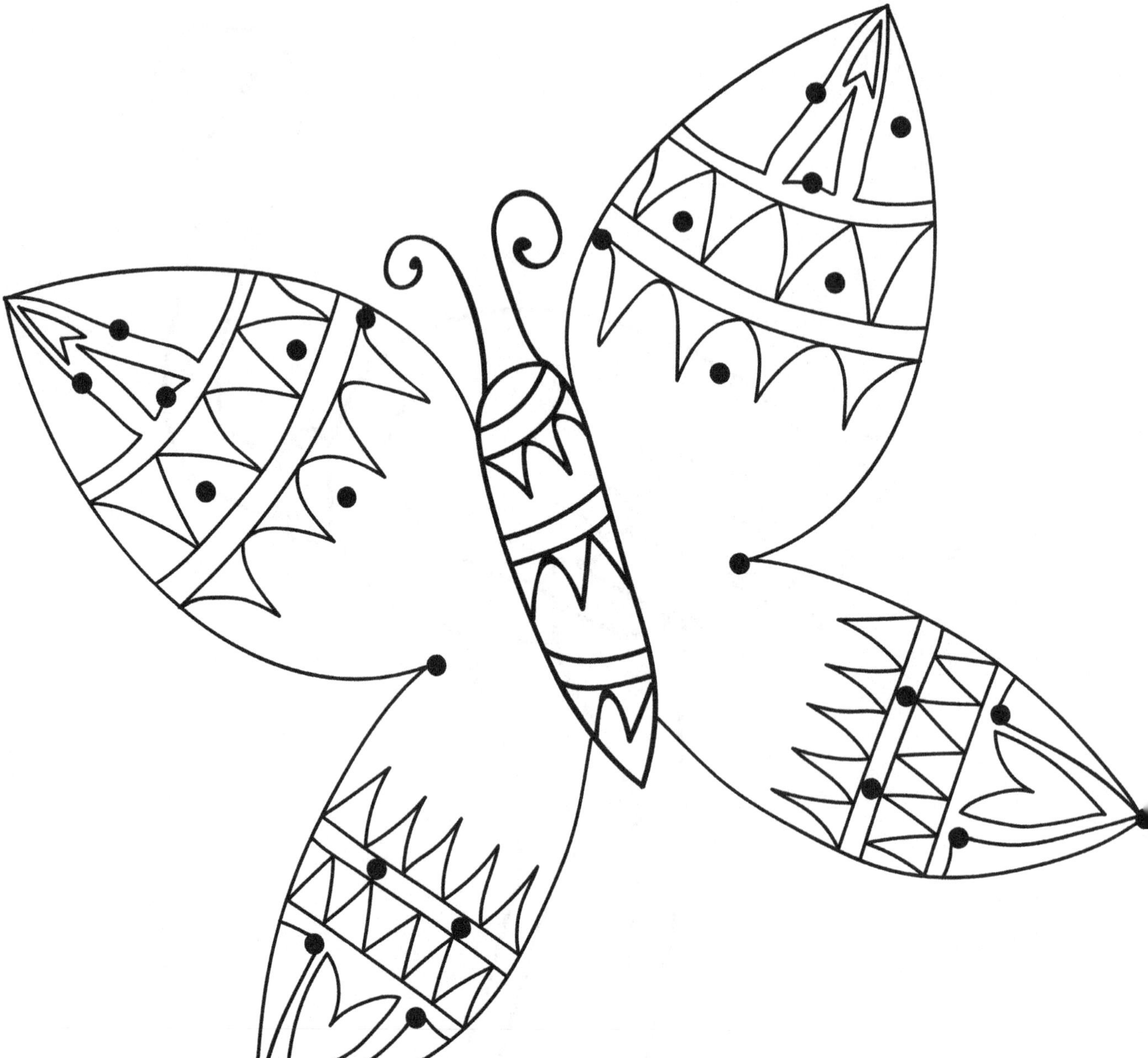

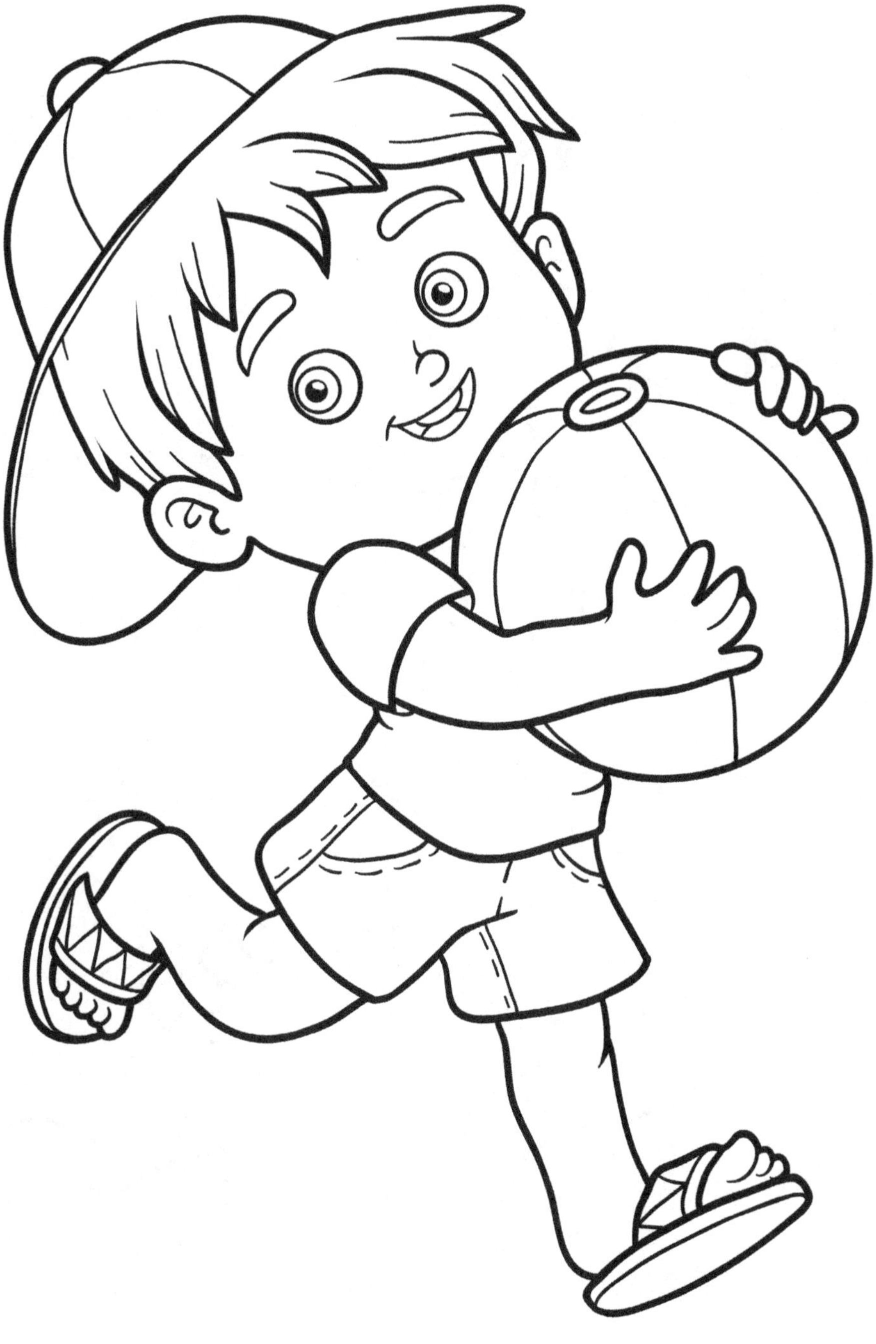

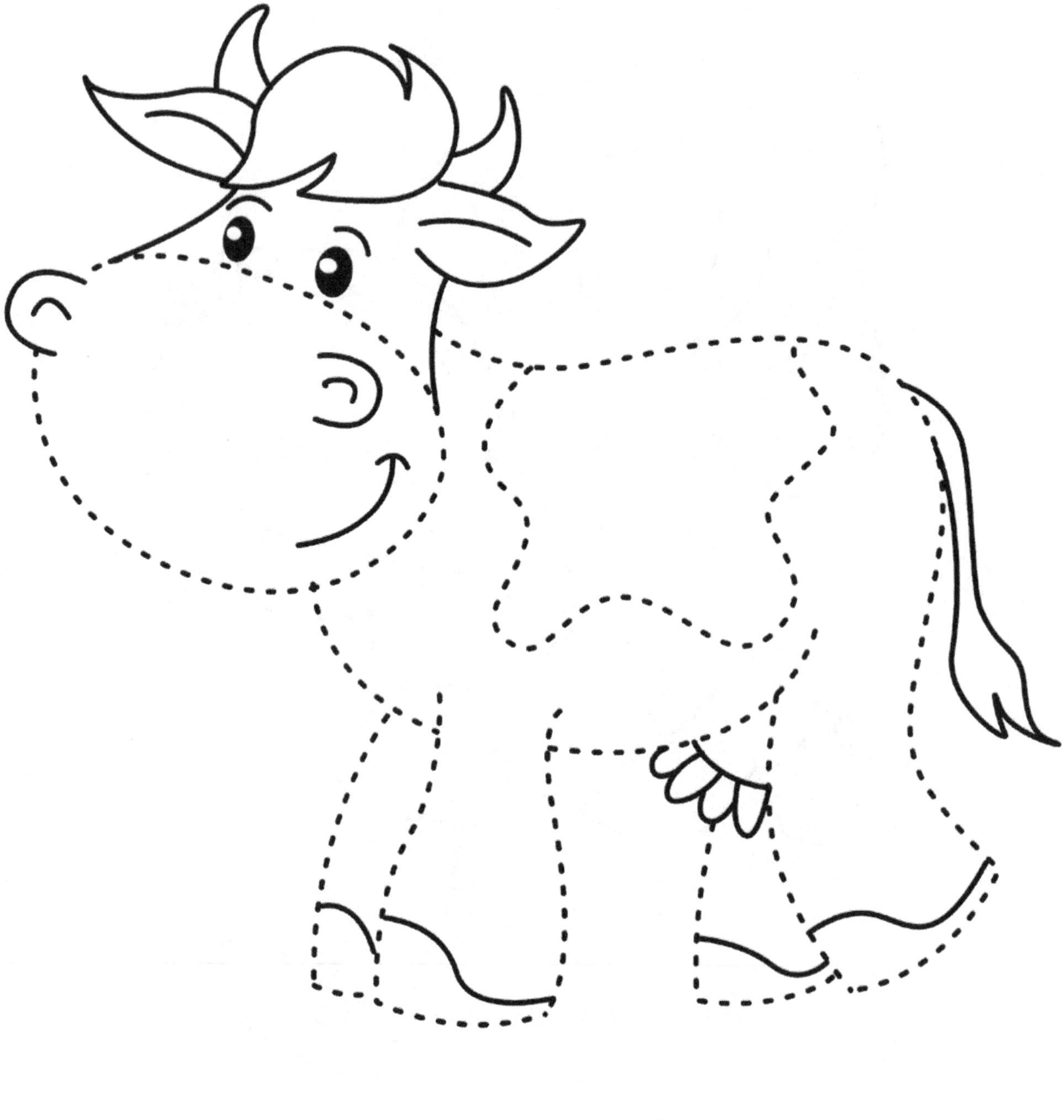

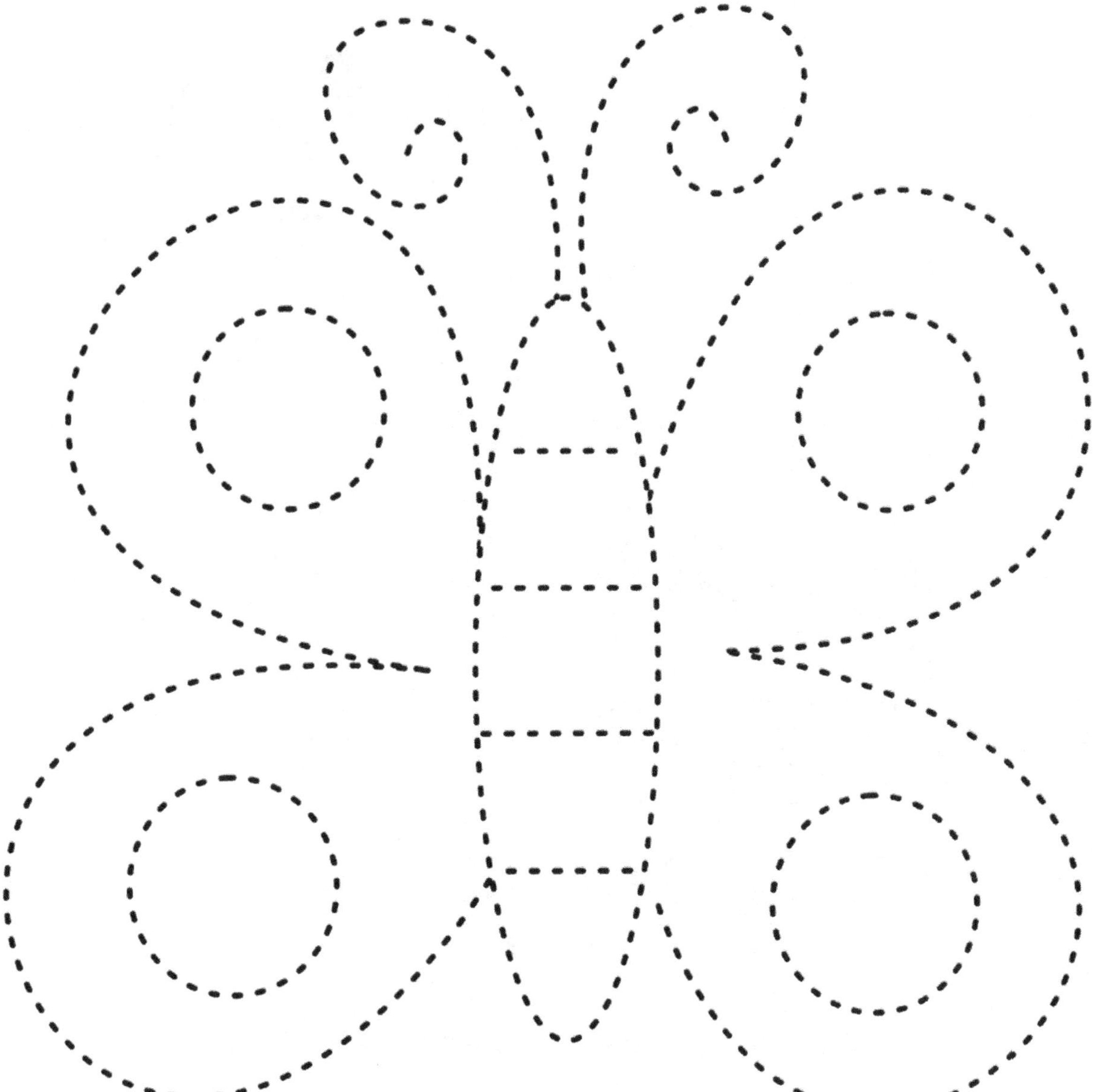

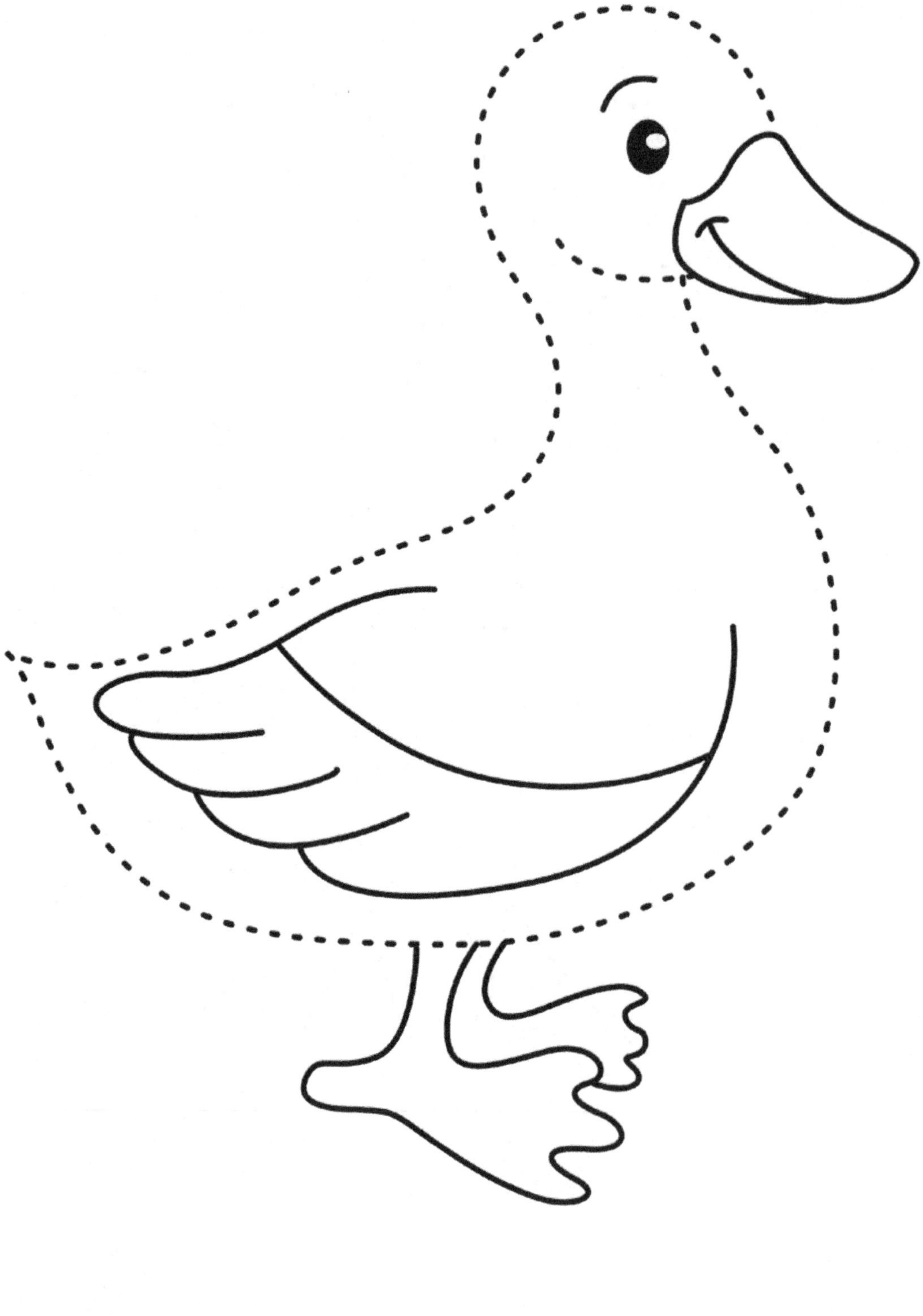

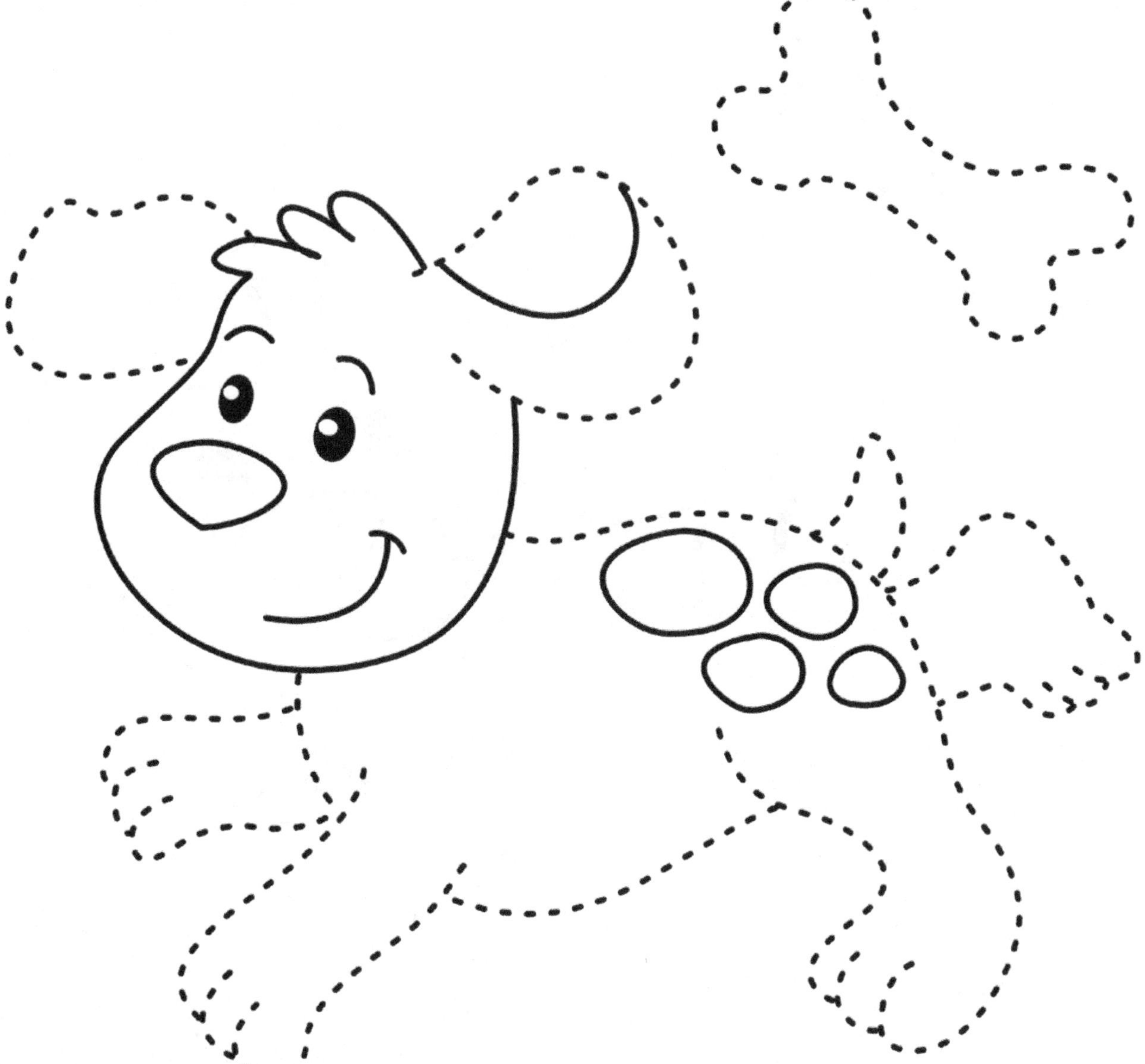

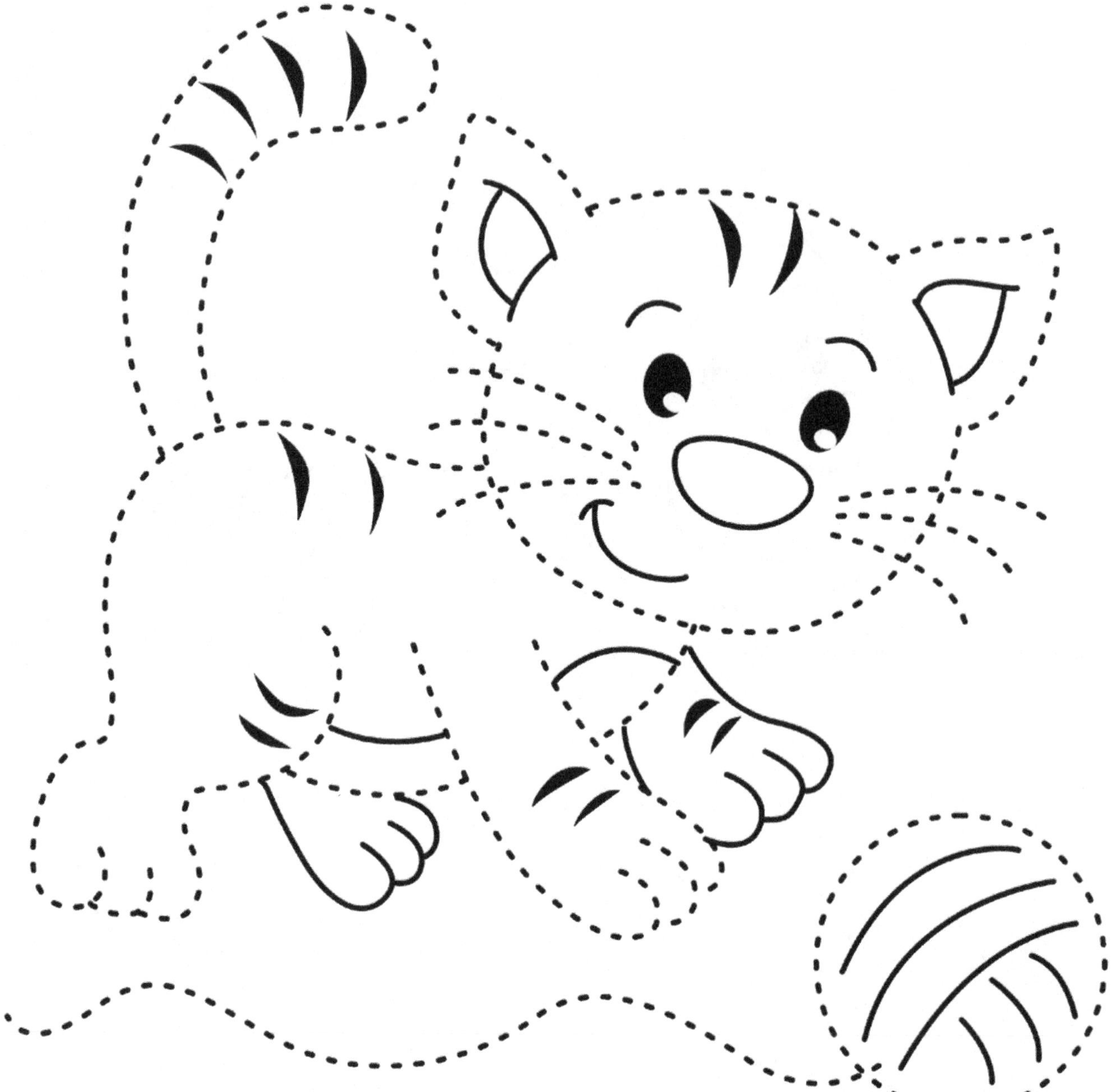

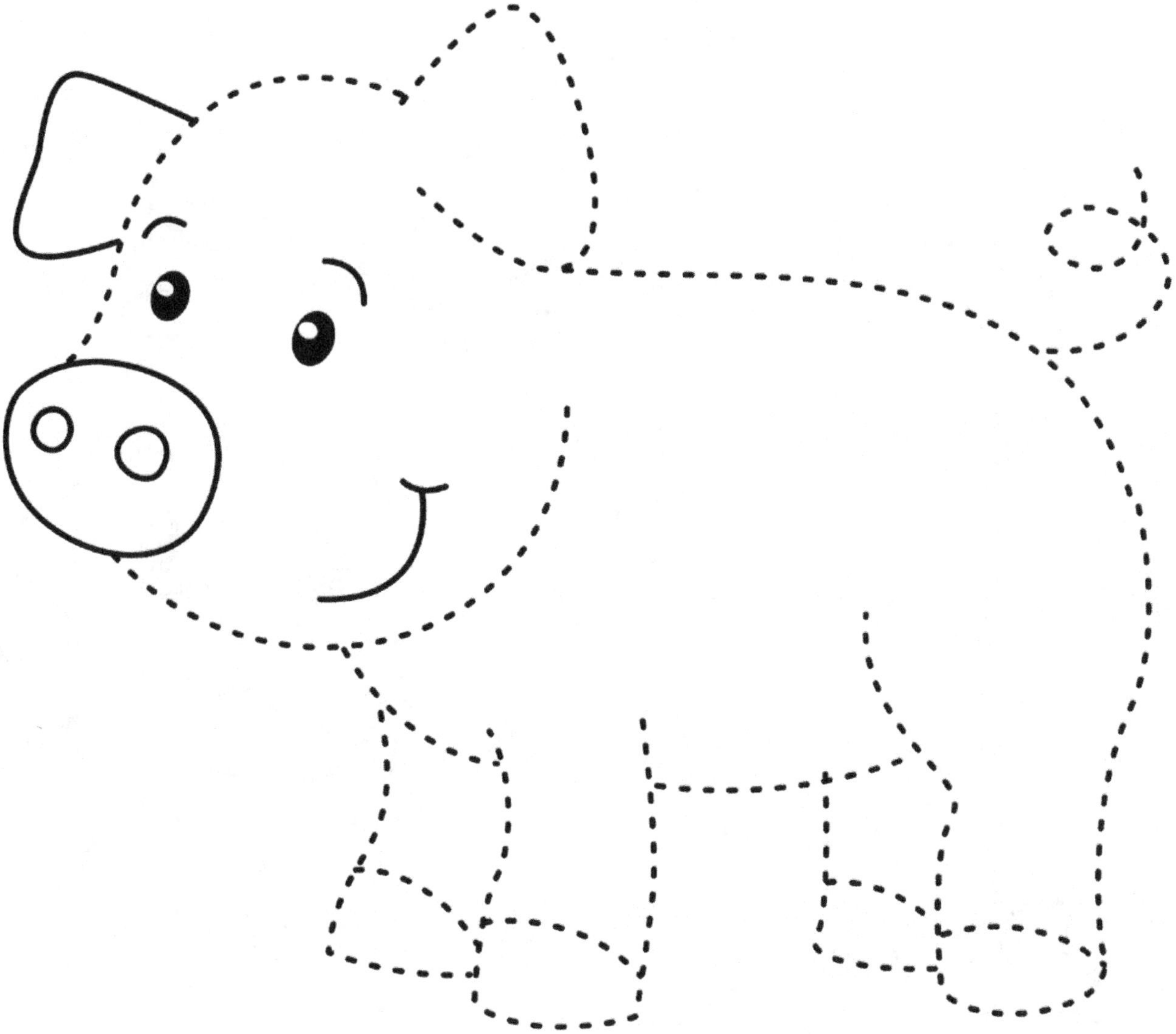

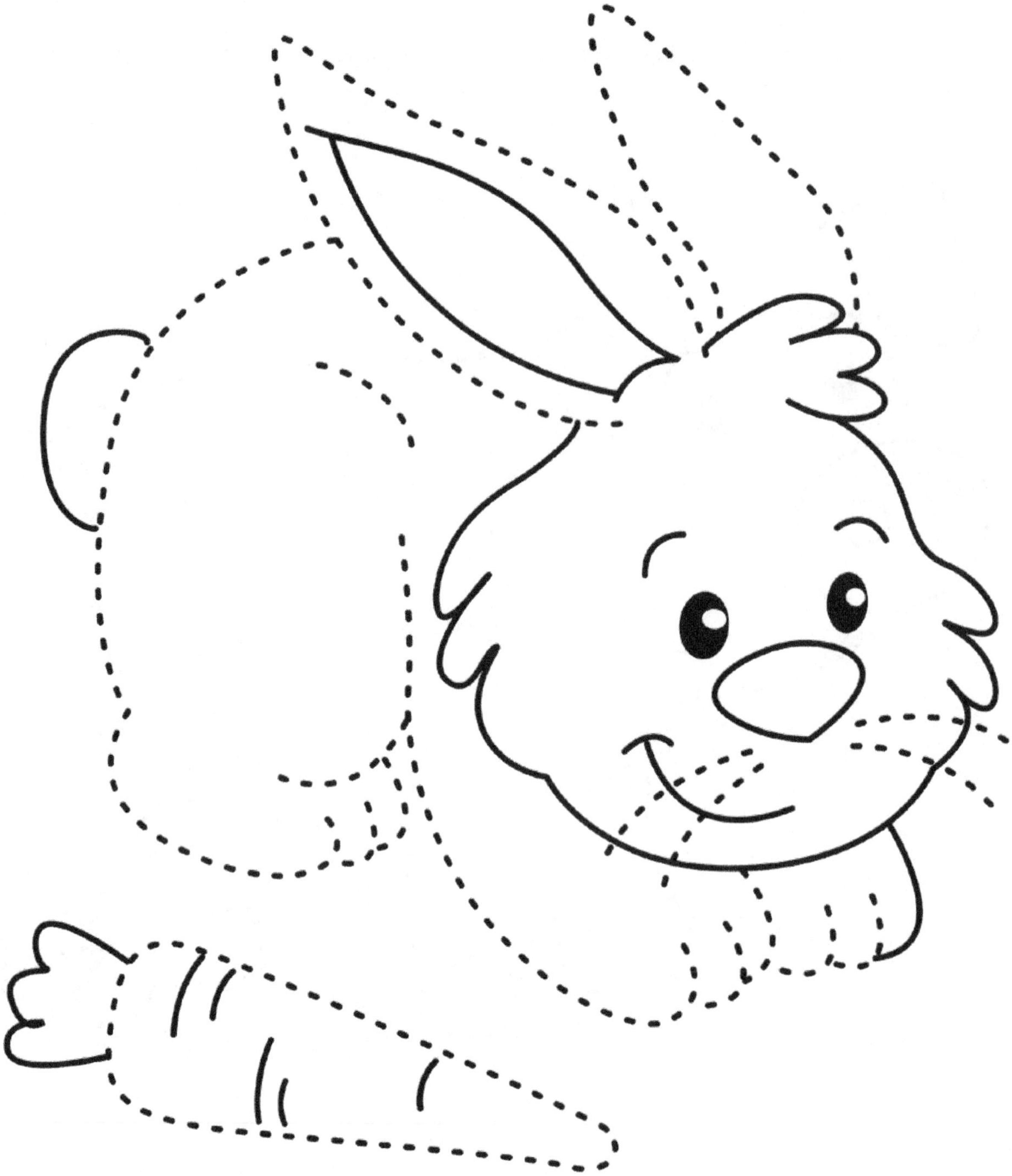

Made in the USA
Coppell, TX
15 February 2020

15565664R00031